DEBRA GABEL

Quilt Blocks Around the World

50 Appliqué Patterns for International Cities & More
Mix & Match to Create Lasting Memories

Where We've Been, 51" × 51", by Patti Rusk

C&T PUBLISHING

Publisher: Amy Marson

Creative Director: Gailen Runge

Acquisitions Editor: Susanne Woods

Editor: Gailen Runge

Book Designer: Kerry Graham

Cover Designer: Kristy Zacharias

Production Coordinator: Zinnia Heinzmann

Production Editor: S. Michele Fry

Photography by Diane Pedersen and Christina Carty-Francis of C&T Publishing, Inc.

Published by C&T Publishing, Inc., P.O. Box 1456, Lafayette, CA 94549

Library of Congress Cataloging-in-Publication Data

Gabel, Debra, 1961-

Quilt blocks around the world : 50 appliqué patterns for international cities & more : mix & match to create lasting memories / Debra Gabel.

p. cm.

ISBN 978-1-60705-435-1 (soft cover)

1. Appliqué--Patterns. 2. Quilting--Patterns. 3. Cities and towns in art. I. Title.

TT779.G33 2012

746.44'5--dc23

2011031347

Printed in China

10 9 8 7 6 5 4 3 2 1

Las Vegas Block, 12″ × 12″

Another Day in Paradise, by Stephanie De Abreu

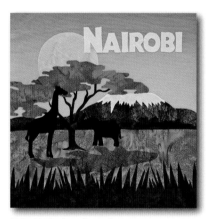

Nairobi Block, 12″ × 12″

Singapore Block, 12″ × 12″

Detail of *British Isles*, page 72

Dedication

I would like to dedicate this book to my father, Arthur James Ogden, who passed away on January 25, 2011, at the age of 84. My dad was a man's man, and he had a great spirit. He was incredibly kind, helpful, and generous with his time. My dad was extremely resourceful and creative. He was proud of me and of my accomplishments. My dad served in the Army and has been to many of the cities in this book. He returned to several of the European cities with my mom after he retired, but as a tourist and not as a soldier. With much love and respect, I dedicate this book to you, Dad!

Acknowledgments

It is hard to believe that I am sitting at my computer writing acknowledgments for this new book just 12 months after my first book, *Quilt Blocks Across America,* was sent to C&T Publishing! I would like to thank C&T Publishing, and especially Susanne Woods, Gailen Runge, Zinnia Heinzmann, and Amy Marson, for being so kind and professional in providing this opportunity. The writing and production were painless with C&T's help.

I must send out a huge acknowledgment to my studio assistant, Patti Rusk. Patti has teenagers and comes to the studio a few days a week. We work well together and commiserate on the trials and tribulations of raising teenagers. I must say we have a grand time! Patti has helped me every step of the way with this book, serving as my sounding board and helping prepare samples for sewing and appliqué by our satellite studio assistant, Mindy Williams. I would design each city block and choose the fabrics. Patti would then cut, iron, and fuse the pieces, as well as sew up a few of the blocks.

Mindy Williams is my quilting goddess! Mindy was a students in a class I taught in Philadelphia a few years back. I ran into her again in the spring of 2010 in her home state of Delaware. One thing led to another, and Mindy agreed to sew and raw-edge appliqué the blocks Patti and I put together. Mindy is a master sewer! Her stitches are impeccable. I am so thankful to have the honor of working with these two ladies doing what I love to do. Mindy is an inspiration and has a pretty terrific husband, Rick.

A big thank-you to Hilda Ogden, my mom, who hand bound the edges of the quilts we made for this book. Mom is not really into quilting, but she did a great job on the bindings. She helps whenever she can in the studio with ironing, binding, stuffing patterns, and keeping all the pins artistically arranged in the pincushions.

The Yahoo World Blocks online volunteer group, many of whose members I have never met, has been exceptional in providing samples, pattern testing, editing of instructions, and input. Many of the volunteers' samples appear in the Gallery (pages 71–77). Quilters who participated in *Quilt Blocks Across America* made several of the gallery entries. My new friend from the group, Lee Hofstetter, has made especially amazing samples. Special thanks to Lee! I can see a long-term friendship blossoming here. Meeting talented new quilters while creating the books I have written has been so rewarding.

Lastly, I would like to thank all the guilds and quilt shops that have invited me to lecture and lead workshops. You are all part of the success of these patterns, and you all played a critical role in helping me zero in on this companion book of world cities that C&T Publishing would bring to market. Everyone's kindness and positive energy are sincerely appreciated.

Contents

Cities with Stripes, 57" × 57", by Debra Gabel, Patti Rusk, Mindy Williams, and Maria O'Haver

World Chain, 74″ × 74″, by Debra Gabel, Patti Rusk, Mindy Williams, and Maria O'Haver

Preface

This is my second quilting book, and I must say the journey progressed more smoothly this time. I knew what to expect and planned better. Writing a book, especially a book that has so many patterns, can seem like a daunting task. With the support of my studio assistants and online sample makers, the book progressed in an orderly and efficient way.

My quilting pattern company, Zebra Patterns, offers more than 100 commercial patterns, and my first book, *Quilt Blocks Across America,* contains 51 patterns. The success of *Quilt Blocks Across America* has made this book possible, which brings my pattern count to well over 200. This second book by C&T seemed like a natural follow-up to *Quilt Blocks Across America.* Now quilters can make ancestry quilts, travel memory quilts, and even bucket list quilts that span the globe!

The whole concept of destination quilts started at Pittsburgh's spring 2009 International Quilt Market, the initial venue for launching the Zebra Patterns line nationally. The patterns were well received by quilt shops, publishers, and fabric companies, with particular attention paid to the CityStamp, StateStamp, NationStamp, and GetAwayStamp patterns. My stamp patterns are unique renditions of extra-large postage stamps that were totally concocted in my head. These stamp patterns made it clear to me that quilters want to make quilts that reflect their lives and travels. *Quilt Blocks Across America* made the 50 states accessible, and now the world blocks make the whole world available to include in special memory quilts. *Quilt Blocks Across America* provided positioning templates, color layouts, a CD with paper patterns, and a large gallery. *Quilt Blocks Around the World* has been set up in the same format so that quilters can use both books to chronicle and visually answer the question, "Where ya been?"

The initial spark that led to *Quilt Blocks Across America* naturally progressed to these world block designs. I cannot tell you how many people asked if I thought I would do other countries. I had already been "baking" the idea of countries or world destinations in my head before I finished the U.S. state blocks.

I thought long and hard about what imagery to include in the second book's blocks. My original thought was to create "country" blocks. I quickly discovered that other countries, like the United States, are extremely diverse within their borders. I did not think I could do a whole country justice in a six-inch-square quilt block. Quickly my attention turned toward international cities and destinations. I felt confident that I could capture the flavor of world destinations by focusing on notable landmarks. That is the intention of this book: to capture the flavor of each destination in six inches of cloth.

Once I zeroed in on the book's concept, I needed to pick the top world destinations. That was no simple task. Of course I started with the obvious, like London, Paris, New York, and Tokyo. There were twelve to fifteen "must have" cities, but then the next level of decisions became a bit more difficult. Once I had the top 30 or so cities chosen, it became a research project to figure out where most world travelers go and to include destinations all over the world. I did ample research on the Internet about the top 50 international travel destinations. I cross-referenced and reassured myself that the top 30 were the right choices. The criteria for the last 20 were set once I looked up and read about each city and its landmarks. If the city had great landmarks that could be translated into cloth, it made the list. C&T acquisitions editor Susanne Woods and I came up with a brilliant idea for how to really be sure we had chosen well. We thought C&T should send us to every destination in the book, plus those under consideration, to ensure that we brought great cities to you, the quilter. Somehow we never got around to formally proposing the idea to Amy Marson, the publisher, for approval. Ha! I told many of my friends and students about the idea. They all agreed but thought it would be better if I took them instead of Susanne! I have been to only a few of the cities in the book and now have many more to add to my bucket list.

Each project begins with a short paragraph overview of the city featured in the block and its notable characteristics and landmarks. Researching the cities took me to each destination for a short while, at least in my imagination. We live in a fascinating world, with so many amazing human contributions that are master works of art. You will see many architectural feats throughout that are stunning, but they do have many small details, such as windows and doors. Be sure to read the Embellishing Small Pieces section (page 8) to keep you out of the insane asylum after doing scores of tiny windows and details. The blocks were designed at six inches to get as many great designs in one book as we could. I strongly recommend enlarging the patterns up to at least eight inches. That said, I blew up my blocks 200 percent to twelve inches, which made the pieces much more manageable.

Translucent Patterning, the same unique process introduced in *Quilt Blocks Across America,* allows the quilter to trace each piece *and* see color, positioning, and overlap all in one block. Imagine looking down through the roof of a building with X-ray vision, and you will get the idea. A CD with digital PDF representations of each block's pattern pieces is included for added ease of use. My sincere hope is that your journey with the patterns in this book is a fun and exciting way for you to respond in cloth to the question, "Where ya been?"

How to Use This Book

Quilt Blocks Around the World presents primarily raw-edge fused appliqué patterns with general directions for use, plus several tips and suggestions. You will find 50 patterns: 46 for international destination cities and four general world blocks. The page layouts are consistent throughout. The cities are listed alphabetically starting on page 19. The world blocks are separate, starting on page 66. The patterns are all designed as 6″ × 6″ finished blocks, but *I strongly suggest that you consider enlarging the designs for ease of use.* The larger the block size, the bigger the small pieces will be. You may hand turn the designs if you are a hand turner. You can enlarge the designs by using the included CD or by making an enlarged color copy at any office products retailer or copy shop, or even at a growing number of public libraries. Keep in mind that you can enlarge the designs onto two pages and tape them together should you want a larger width than the standard 8½″ × 11″ sheet of paper. On page 2 you will find a "permission to copy" statement for copy shops.

I strongly suggest that you consider enlarging the designs for ease of use.

Descriptive and Directions Paragraphs

Each block's page starts with a brief descriptive paragraph, making reference to notable facts about the city and the images in the pattern. The next paragraph gives simple general instructions, followed by creative suggestions, if applicable, to enhance that particular block. If the simple directions on each pattern page are not informative enough for you, please read the entire General Block Directions chapter (pages 12–15), which describes how to assemble the blocks. By following the block directions and using the creative suggestions, you will be able to make a beautiful international block for your personalized quilt or project. You can always write to me at debra@zebrapatterns.com with any questions. You can also combine these blocks with blocks from *Quilt Blocks Across America*. The blocks in the two books are scaled the same to allow easy combining of U.S. and international destinations.

Read each block's directions paragraph carefully. Each paragraph starts with general piecing and fusing instructions, followed by embellishment suggestions or alternative ways to create some of the details, when applicable.

About the Block Designs: Mix, Match, and Edit

You can easily edit any block to your particular experience. Maybe your experience at a world destination was more about a beach than urban sightseeing. You could take the Caribbean block and insert "San Juan" to represent your Puerto Rico beach experience. You could add a favorite element from another block to the new block you are creating. Or maybe, as another example, you went to other destinations in France in addition to Paris. You could replace "Paris" with "France," include just the Eiffel Tower, and mix it with some countryside elements. Feel free to mix and match to better represent your response to "Where ya been?"

Feel free to mix and match graphics from other blocks to make your block ring more true to your vision of the answer to "Where ya been?"

Use most of the Caribbean Block and flip elements.

Remove the sand castle and chair.

Change fabric colors.

Use the type from San Juan.

Take the tortoise and rocks from the Galapagos Islands and flip pieces.

Mix and match to create a new block!

Creating Block Backgrounds for All Blocks

Throughout this book, most of the 6½˝ × 6½˝ unfinished patterns will have a 3½˝ × 6¾˝ sky piece sewn to a 4½˝ × 6¾˝ land piece to make up the background of the block. The unfinished pieced block should be 7½˝ tall × 6¾˝ wide; the extra background will allow you to position the seamline and trim the block to exactly 6½˝ square. The seam between the land and sky needs to be a standard ¼˝, pressed toward the darker fabric. A few blocks have solid backgrounds, which should be cut as 7˝ × 7˝ squares. You will place the fused appliqué pieces on either the pieced background or the full square background to complete the block.

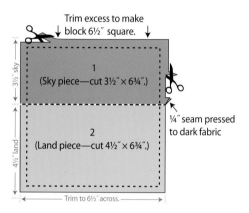

Trim excess to make block 6½˝ square.

3½˝ sky

1
(Sky piece—cut 3½˝ × 6¾˝.)

¼˝ seam pressed to dark fabric

4½˝ land

2
(Land piece—cut 4½˝ × 6¾˝.)

Trim to 6½˝ across.

Numbering of Pattern Pieces

The sky and land pattern pieces are always numbered 1 and 2 respectively. The remaining elements are numbered in the order in which they are to be assembled. Piece 3 will be positioned after the background is created, unless otherwise noted, and will then be followed by pieces 4, 5, and so on.

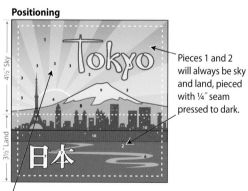

Positioning

4½˝ Sky

3½˝ Land

Pieces 1 and 2 will always be sky and land, pieced with ¼˝ seam pressed to dark.

After background is done, position pieces in numeric order (after background, position 3, then 4 …).

PATTERN PIECES WITHOUT NUMBERS

Some of the smallest details, such as windows and doors, may not have numbers. This indicates that the pieces would be translated easier via thread or fabric paint. Some of these details can even be eliminated if you feel they are just too small. These small objects become more manageable after the pattern has been enlarged. By enlarging the 6˝ block 200 percent, a tiny ¼˝ window becomes a more manageable ½˝ piece.

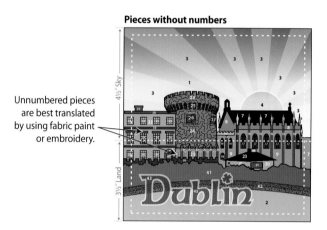

Pieces without numbers

4½˝ Sky

3½˝ Land

Unnumbered pieces are best translated by using fabric paint or embroidery.

EMBELLISHING SMALL PIECES

Sewing on decorative beading can be effective for some of the small details, such as windows and doors. On many of the buildings, small bars of trim separate portions of the structures. Decorative lace works well in these areas. Often I use readily available fabric paint or markers from craft stores to paint or draw tiny details. Just be sure the paint or markers you use are made for fabric. Using products not especially made for cloth can result in bleeding colors, cracking, or other undesirable effects. Fabric glitter is yet another method for adding a bit of embellishment to your projects. The key to embellishment is to use it sparingly. Overuse of embellishments can quickly lead to tacky results.

Translucent Patterning and Tracing

All the patterns have been drawn with translucent overlapping color in order to show how the pieces fit together. Look carefully at the pieces and then trace the outline of each numbered piece. The translucency allows you to see the overlap of the drawn pieces. *Do not use the pattern colors for fabric choices.* Refer to the small picture adjacent to the city paragraphs and to the block directions at the top of each page for color recommendations. You will be tracing each numbered element separately onto tracing paper. If you do not want to trace, all the pieces are separated on the included CD in PDF format.

Translucent patterns for tracing

Pieces are translucent for tracing each overlapping appliqué piece. *Do not use* for color reference.

Trace and number pattern pieces onto tracing paper.

Trace each element onto tracing paper and write number on traced piece.

100% color patterns for fabric selection

Smaller illustration adjacent to written paragraphs on each page is 100% color for fabric choices.

Special Pattern Element

A complete image of the Las Vegas sign for the Las Vegas block (page 41) is included on the CD also. This element was included separately because it is intricate and difficult to trace and translate into pieces. The detailed significance is so meaningful that it should appear in cloth as accurately as possible. The Vegas sign is in one piece on the CD and can be printed onto printable fabric. Once the Vegas sign is printed and fused following the manufacturer's instructions, you can use it as you would any other element in the block. The pattern pieces also have been provided for those brave quilters who love a challenge.

City Names

When I was designing this book, I decided to use a different font for each international city, unlike in my last book, *Quilt Blocks Across America*, which has state abbreviations all in the same font. Using various fonts further enhanced the setting of the blocks. Some of the typefaces are challenging not only to cut but also to stitch. You might use commercial fusible lettering or computer-generated typography, or embroider the letters by hand or machine using a similar font.

Tips

TIP 1: If you have an embroidery unit on your sewing machine, you could embroider the letters using a similar font found in your software.

TIP 2: You could cut out the city name type and stitch it on with quilt-shop-quality invisible thread, thereby minimizing the necessary accuracy around complex curves and shapes. The invisible thread will keep the appliqué down, and the thread will not show, allowing just the cut fabric to define the lettering edges.

TIP 3: Creating your own two-color type on a computer and printing the letters on printable fabric is yet another way to make the type on each city block.

TIP 4: You could use commercially available fusible lettering.

Raw-Edge Sewing

Sewing the raw edges of the appliqué pieces is both a functional and an aesthetic task. Functionally, stitching down the raw edges holds the pieces in place and minimizes edge fraying. Aesthetically, sewing down the raw edges is an opportunity to add another design element through color or stitch choice. Raw-edge sewing will reflect your own personal choices. If you want the edging to blend, use matching-color threads. If an added noticeable line is desired, use a contrasting thread. The length and width of your zigzag stitching are also matters of personal taste. I use a somewhat narrow, tight zigzag, which I often describe as a dense zigzag or a slightly open satin stitch. You can also use a decorative or blanket stitch to hold the edges down. Again, it is all subjective. I would recommend making a small test sample using fused scraps to try out your raw-edge stitch. Sew a few inches of the fused scrap piece and examine the stitching to ensure that you are satisfied with the results before starting the real block.

Anchor the stitching by sewing three stitches in place with the sewing machine. Then the zigzagging begins. When sewing the zigzag edging, it is important to position the stitching so that the outermost part of the stitch just pierces the underlying fabric. The main "bite" of the stitch stays on the cut pattern piece. If you straddle the pattern piece edge, you will see the zigging edges on the underlying fabric. If you miss the edge and zig only on the pattern piece, you will leave a sliver of unfinished fabric edging that will be prone to fraying. Try to pierce just outside the pattern piece edge. At the end of the zigzag stitching, I again anchor the stitching by sewing three stitches in place with the sewing machine.

Anchor by sewing in place 3 times.

Pattern piece

Use matching thread and pierce edge of underlying fabric.

Underlying fabric

PRESSER FOOT: Using an open-toe presser foot on your sewing machine will help with edge stitching accuracy. Also, if your sewing machine has a needle-position adjustment, move the needle position to the far right. Use the right prong of the open-toe sewing foot to follow the right edge of the fabric, providing accurate stitch placement. See diagram (at right).

THREADS: Using good thread is essential to any quality sewing project. Many retail chain stores and discount department stores carry inexpensive threads. Avoid these threads at all cost! The thread is the "glue" in your project. If you use cheap threads, the glue will come undone quickly as well as be detrimental to your sewing machine. There are many quality threads on the market today. Your local quilt shop will be able to guide you to strong, beautiful, clean threads. A printed number on each spool of thread indicates the weight of the thread. Higher thread numbers are finer threads. For example, a 60- or 100-weight thread will be very fine. A 40-weight thread is standard. A 30-weight or 12-weight thread is heavy.

I typically use a combination of threads. I use a thin thread in my bobbin, usually a 60-weight. This has two major benefits. The first is that it allows the top thread (I typically use a 40-weight thread) to lie on top of the project better. The second is that with finer thread, you can get many more yards on the bobbin spool, making bobbin changes less frequent. If I am submitting a competition quilt, I will match the top and bottom thread colors. White, black, and medium gray or tan will suffice for most projects.

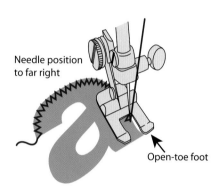

Needle position to far right

Open-toe foot

Tips

TIP 1: Use an open-toe presser foot for visibility of zigzag stitching.

TIP 2: If your sewing machine has an adjustable needle position, move the needle to the far right. That allows you to ride the edge with the right prong of the open-toe foot and easily keep the stitching on the edge.

TIP 3: Use a thin thread (60- to 100-weight) on the bobbin and a 30- to 40-weight top thread to allow the heavier thread to lie nicely on the quilt top. Also, the thinner bobbin thread lasts twice as long as the 30- to 40-weight top thread.

TIP 4: Use a 70/10, 80/12, or 90/14 Microtex needle for raw-edge sewing. Changing needles frequently will also improve your stitch quality.

RAW-EDGE ZIGZAG CORNERS, POINTS, AND CURVES

OUTER CORNERS: When sewing raw-edge outer corners, zigzag to the corner edges. Stop sewing when the needle is in the down position on the pattern piece's outer edge. Then pivot the work. Begin sewing again, crossing the first stitches. You might need to hand turn the sewing machine wheel and slightly adjust the fabric to get the needle in the right position so it pivots in the corner.

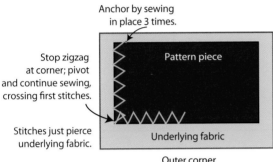

Anchor by sewing in place 3 times.

Stop zigzag at corner; pivot and continue sewing, crossing first stitches.

Pattern piece

Stitches just pierce underlying fabric.

Underlying fabric

Outer corner

INNER CORNERS: When sewing raw-edge inner corners, zigzag to the inner corner. Stop sewing when the needle is in the down position on the pattern piece's outer edge. Then pivot the work. Begin sewing again. There will not be any stitches in the inner corner area.

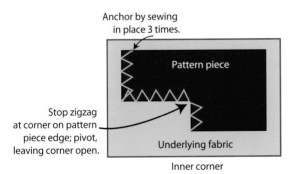

Anchor by sewing in place 3 times.

Pattern piece

Stop zigzag at corner on pattern piece edge; pivot, leaving corner open.

Underlying fabric

Inner corner

CURVES: When sewing raw-edge curves, going slowly is critical. Sew one or two stitches, stop with the needle down, and then pivot. The number of stitches and the degree of pivoting depend on the tightness and size of the curve. The goal is to keep the zigzag stitches even throughout the curve.

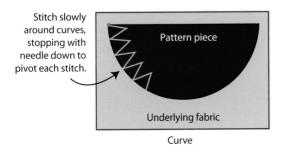

Stitch slowly around curves, stopping with needle down to pivot each stitch.

Pattern piece

Underlying fabric

Curve

POINTS: When sewing raw-edge points, it is necessary to decrease the stitch width as you approach the end of the point. End at the point with the needle down, and then reverse the stitch by slowly increasing the stitch width until the stitch is back to the original width.

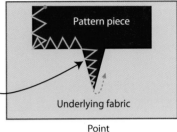

Gradually decrease the stitch width into the point. End at point with needle down; pivot and reverse up other side of point.

Pattern piece

Underlying fabric

Point

Using Organza or Tulle for Shadows or Sun Rays

Some of the patterns in this book have shadows, while others have subtle sun rays. These items are optional. Using white organza or tulle for the sun rays will produce a light, translucent effect. Using a dark-colored organza or tulle for shadows generally works well. These items are enhancements that can be left off the block if you want to simplify it.

When working with organza or tulle, proceed in the same manner as you would for creating fabric pattern pieces. Mistyfuse Ultraviolet fusible is excellent for the fusible backing. It is very light and will maintain the sheer fabric's translucent properties. The ultraviolet version protects the pieces from discoloring over time.

Organza and tulle are sheer, open-weave fiber products. When you apply fusible webbing to the back, it will bleed through to some extent. This makes using a nonstick pressing sheet essential. I prefer the 21˝ × 27˝ Fat Goddess Sheet for appliqué pressing.

I have found that high iron temperatures can melt or scorch organza and tulle more quickly than other fabrics. Determine and then use the lowest iron setting necessary to fuse. Once these translucent pieces are in place, always use a pressing sheet if further ironing is needed; this will prevent melting or scorching.

General Block Directions

Materials Needed

Fabrics chosen for particular block

Fusible webbing

Nonstick appliqué pressing sheet

Sharp pair of cutting scissors

Rotary cutter

Quilting ruler

Good, clean iron

Copy machine

Tracing pad and pencil

Lightbox (helpful for tracing, but not necessary)

Sewing machine with open-toe foot

Matching threads for all elements

Tear-away stabilizer for appliqué sewing

Batting

Clean work space

Block Directions

1. Create the block background.

Cut a 3½˝ × 6¾˝ sky (or land) piece and a 4½˝ × 6¾˝ land (or sky) piece. Use the small color graphic block on each pattern page for your fabric choice color reference. Sew the pieces together with a standard ¼˝ seam. *These pieces do not have fusible webbing on the back.* This will make up the background of each block. Press the seams toward the dark fabric. You will place the fused appliqué pieces on this pieced background to complete the block. (Refer to Creating Block Backgrounds for All Blocks on page 8.) Note: A few blocks have solid backgrounds, which do not require any preparation.

Tip

The background rectangles for the sky and land are generous (6¾˝ wide) so that you can trim the block to 6½˝ square. When trimming, be sure to position the seamline correctly according to the layout.

2. Trace each numbered element separately onto tracing paper. Be sure to write the number onto the traced piece matching the pattern. (Refer to Translucent Patterning and Tracing on page 9.) If you choose to use the CD, simply print out pattern sheets at the desired scale. CD patterns are prenumbered.

Tip

You might want to jot down the color of the traced piece to help in matching fabric and assembly.

3. Rough cut out all the traced pattern pieces and separate the individual traced pieces into piles based on the colors to be used.

Rough cut traced pattern pieces of same color.

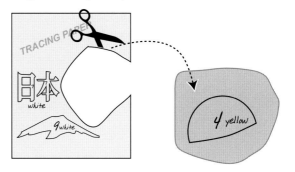

Tip

Remember, there is no need to cut the traced or printed CD patterns on exact lines at this time. Just rough cut each piece.

4. Take a pile of like-colored pattern pieces and lay them out on the actual fabric to get a rough idea of how much fabric you will need. Position the pieces close together, but not overlapping, to use the fabric efficiently. With sharp scissors, rough cut enough fabric to allow all the pieces to fit on the chosen fabric. Set the traced pieces aside and make a pile of "to be fused" fabrics. You will fuse all the rough cuts at one time for efficiency.

Place same color pattern pieces on fabric choice and rough cut block of fabric to be fused.

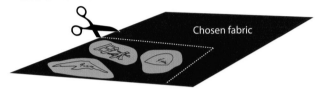

5. Once you have rough cut all the fabrics, you are ready to fuse. Lay out enough fusible webbing to accommodate all the fabric pieces.

6. Sandwich the fabric with fusible webbing in between nonstick appliqué pressing sheets to protect your iron and ironing surface.

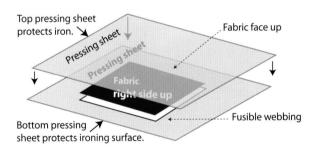

Top pressing sheet protects iron.
Fabric face up
Fabric right side up
Fusible webbing
Bottom pressing sheet protects ironing surface.

7. Following the manufacturer's instructions for heat and timing, fuse the fabric swatches to the webbing. Iron the top of the nonstick pressing sheet sandwich; then flip and iron the opposite side. Applying heat from both sides ensures a good bond of the fusible webbing to the fabric.

8. Let the nonstick appliqué sandwich cool before removing the fused fabric. Clean off any fusible webbing debris left behind on the pressing sheets.

9. Rough cut the fused fabrics apart.

10. Rematch the rough-cut pattern pieces with the correct fused fabric swatches.

11. Pin all rough-cut pattern pieces *right side up* to the appropriate fused fabric, also *right side up*.

Pin rough-cut pattern pieces to right side of chosen fabric.

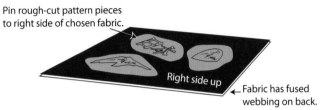

Right side up
Fabric has fused webbing on back.

Tip

Small pieces can be held in place with temporary glue, low-adhesive tape, or a small spot of double-sided tape.

12. With sharp scissors, carefully cut out each pattern piece on the traced lines or on the pattern lines if the pieces were printed from the CD. After all the patterns are cut, you will be ready to position. *Do not remove the pins or backing* yet.

13. Position the pattern pieces by referring to the numbered translucent pattern as your guide. Remove the pins and backing from each piece as you go. Position the pieces numerically, starting with piece 3. (*Reminder:* Pieces 1 and 2 are the sky and land pieces.)

Do not try to remove fused backing by picking at the edges or corners. Simply take a pin and score the back of the pattern piece in the middle. Gently bend the score until the backing separates. Then tear it away from the middle. You do not want to fray the fabric by picking at the corners or edges.

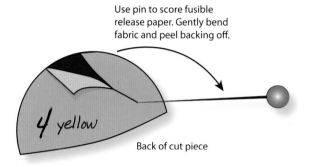

Use pin to score fusible release paper. Gently bend fabric and peel backing off.

4 yellow

Back of cut piece

14. Once the block is in position, lay a clean appliqué pressing sheet over the top and fuse all the elements in place, following the manufacturer's instructions. If the fusible you are using requires steam for the final set, remove the pressing sheet and steam as instructed after the block is pressed into position. The Warm Company's Lite Steam-A-Seam 2 produces the best results for me. Remember that steam cannot penetrate through nonstick appliqué pressing sheets. Once pressed, the block is complete and ready for stitching.

If your project includes organza or tulle, use a muslin cloth barrier in those areas when fusing for the final set. The muslin will protect the organza or tulle but will allow steam to penetrate.

15. The steps for stitching down the fused appliqué depend on the size of the project. I use a somewhat tight, narrow zigzag in my raw-edge appliqué. I often describe this stitch as a dense zigzag or an open satin stitch. Because the density of stitching can cause the fabric to pucker, it's important to stabilize the block. With smaller projects, you can stabilize with the batting; for larger projects, you can use stabilizer, as described below.

SMALL PROJECT: If you have a small project that will be easy to manipulate in your sewing machine, sandwich only the top (which has appliqués that are fused but not yet stitched) and batting at this point. Add borders to the top. Carefully iron the border seams toward the darker fabric. Place a layer of fusible webbing between the top and the batting. I use Mistyfuse. Fuse the top to the batting, ironing in the center first and moving carefully outward toward the edges, avoiding any wrinkles. This step replaces pinning or hand basting. Now the project is fused to the batting, and the batting becomes the stabilizer.

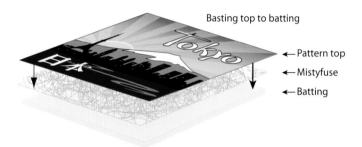

Basting top to batting

← Pattern top

← Mistyfuse

← Batting

When you are sewing, the dense zigzag stitches will be on the back of the batting. After all the raw-edge stitching is complete, cover the batting with the backing before quilting the whole sandwich. You may be wondering whether the batting will sew with ease without fabric on the back. I have found that if you use high-quality low-loft batting, there is no problem. The Warm Company's Warm & Natural needled cotton batting is excellent for this purpose. You just need to clean your machine before or after every sewing session.

LARGE PROJECT: Larger projects are easier to handle if you stitch down the raw-edge appliqué on each block before adding the sashing and borders. There are many stabilizers on the market. I use a tear-away stabilizer. You can also use wash-away stabilizers, stay-in stabilizers, or even freezer paper. Whichever method you choose, you need to stabilize the block before zigging around all the pieces with dense stitching. Once you have stitched down the appliqué on all the blocks, you can add the sashing and borders.

Next you will be ready to add batting. Place a layer of Mistyfuse between the top and the batting. This method of sandwiching will replace hand basting with thread or pins. Then fuse the top to the batting. (Refer to the illustration on page 14.) I start ironing in the center and carefully iron toward the edges to avoid creating wrinkles.

Be sure the top is square. Do not pull the fabric while fusing to avoid distorting the top on the batting. Sometimes this distortion can work to your advantage when you have an area that is warped, but other times, pulling the top can result in undesired effects.

16. Whether your project is small or large, you will now apply the finished raw-edged top and batting to the backing. Place another layer of Mistyfuse under the top / batting and fuse it to the backing. Once again, start ironing in the center and carefully iron toward the edges, avoiding any wrinkles. This method is great for small or large projects in place of basting. It will make a quilt sandwich that is as flat as a pancake, with no pins, plastic, or basting stitches to avoid and remove. The recommended fusing and batting materials will leave the sandwich light, flexible, and easy to work with and care for.

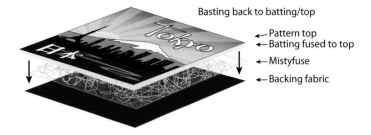

Basting back to batting/top

← Pattern top
← Batting fused to top
← Mistyfuse
← Backing fabric

Be sure the top is square. Do not pull the fabric while fusing to avoid distorting the backing.

17. Quilt your project. I always start quilting by stitching the entire quilt in-the-ditch between the blocks and borders. This generally secures the whole quilt. Next, I quilt in-the-ditch around the feature elements. Last, I work from the center out with custom quilting. The fused sandwich is very stable. You can twist and manipulate the sandwich without any worries of wrinkles or distortion during quilting.

18. Once your whole project is quilted, you can bind and enjoy looking at a wonderful piece that will always remind you of "where ya been."

Put a label on the back with the recipient's name and the name of the quilter, if someone quilted it for you. Include the completion or gifting date. Many of my students have used inkjet-printable fabric and included a written narrative about each block on the label.

Quilt Blocks Around the World

Supplies

As you know, there are many brands of all quilting supplies. I have tried many of these supplies and have come up with the following list as my staples. Of course, as with any project, you can use whatever you feel most comfortable with.

It is important for me to tell you that my supply preferences have evolved over time, independent of any relationships with the manufacturers or suppliers of these products, and they have been chosen based on superior performance and appearance in my projects over the past ten years.

Fabric

I try to use batiks as often as possible. I have found that batiks are more tightly woven and typically fray less than printed fabrics. I have always used fabrics from high-quality quilt shops, even before any shops became customers for my patterns and classes. Hoffman California Fabrics has an extensive line of colored batiks called Bali Hand-dyed Watercolors (Style #1895), which works very well. This Hoffman line has hundreds of colors that are readily available at local quilt stores. These fabrics read as solid prints, yet offer rich batik markings.

Fusible Webbing

I use The Warm Company's Lite Steam-A-Seam 2. This fusible webbing is backed *and* faced with release paper. Most other fusibles have release paper on only one side. The Lite Steam-A-Seam 2 top sheet, when removed, exposes the tacky fusible. The tack is great for holding fabric in position while fusing with a hot iron. Pieces do not slide and move into unwanted positions. This product comes in packages and as yardage on bolts. When the front is fused to the fabric and the back release paper is removed, the back side of the fusible is also tacky. This is great for temporary positioning. (Fusibles that are slick on the back make sliding pieces an issue.) Once all the pieces are in place, you steam them. The steam makes a permanent bond. If you try to remove the pieces after they have been steamed, it will ruin the fabric. This is the kind of permanent hold you want. Having an excellent fuse is very important when doing raw-edge appliqué.

Appliqué Pressing Sheets

I use the Fat Goddess Sheet by the people who manufacture the light, airy Mistyfuse that I recommend for basting. The jumbo pressing sheet, which measures 21″ × 27″, is a translucent tan Teflon sheet that you can see through for positioning. This huge pressing sheet makes a sandwich within which fusing can be done well and easily. I place half the large sheet on my ironing surface and place my ready-to-be-fused pieces and webbing on that half. Then I fold the other half of the pressing sheet on top of the fabric. The top half protects the iron from melted fusible webbing. The bottom half provides the same protection for the ironing surface. Even the most experienced quilter can have a brain freeze and end up with a fused iron surface, which is a real mess! Folding the jumbo pressing sheet in half with fabric and fusing sandwiched in the middle guarantees no mess. I have found that when I sandwich the appliquéd pieces in this manner, I can conveniently and thoroughly iron both the top and the bottom of the sandwich to evenly melt the fusible over every inch of the pattern pieces. If I miss a spot when fusing the top, chances are that I will get it on the back. Ironing both the top and the bottom helps prevent peeling due to fusible that was missed with heat.

Scissors

I use sharp, top-brand scissors. I have a large pair and a small appliqué pair. When you are cutting out small, intricate appliqué pieces, you do not want to be fighting with dull scissors that can fray edges. I get my scissors sharpened twice a year *before* they show wear.

Rotary Cutters

I use a standard rotary cutter and sharp blades. If I get a burr in the cutting wheel, I change the blade immediately. I also use the rotary cutters for making any straight-edged shapes. For example, if I am cutting ten small windows that are the same size, I will cut one long strip with the rotary cutter and then subcut that strip into individual windows. If a building has a square for the main part, I will measure and cut that shape with the rotary cutter. I find it much easier to cut straight lines in this way rather than with scissors.

Sewing Machine

For raw-edge appliqué, any machine that can sew a zigzag and a straight stitch will do. The features that I find very helpful are needle down and knee lift. The needle-down feature allows me to stop stitching with the needle in the down position. This makes for easy pivoting on curves and corners. The knee lift allows me to more quickly loosen the grab of the presser foot for rotation and pivoting. These features are very nice but not necessary.

I do clean my machine each time I sit down to sew. I am a quick worker but would not skip this step. A poorly running machine can be due to lint buildup. Good-quality thread and cleaning will help keep the machine running well. Listen carefully to your sewing machine. As soon as you hear your machine sounding funny, stop. Clean the bobbin area, rethread the top thread, rethread the bobbin, and try again. Many times these simple steps of cleaning and rethreading will stop a problem from developing.

Open-Toe Foot

I use an open-toe foot for my appliqué because it allows me to see the needle piercing the fabric edge with every stitch. In my experience, clear feet distort the edge slightly, making it hard to appliqué right on the edge. Regular feet, with the metal piece surrounding the needle on the foot, obstruct too much of the appliqué to see where you need to be sewing.

Threads

I use only top-quality threads. My projects use YLI, WonderFil, or Madeira threads. These threads will not cause lint buildup on the working parts of the machine, thus preventing inoperability or, worse, damage.

Sometimes I use invisible threads from either Sew-Art International or YLI. Invisible threads are great when they work. In my experience, these two brands are the most reliable invisible threads. Using invisible threads from chain stores will typically result in a trip to the sewing machine repair shop!

I generally use 40-weight polyester embroidery threads in the top, which provide luster to finished projects. I typically use a lighter 60-weight bobbin thread, which allows the top thread to lie on the surface better. Matching the top and bobbin thread colors is your best bet for avoiding tension picking. That said, to save time, I do often use white, black, medium gray, or tan bobbin thread with a colored top thread. I match the color value—light with white, medium with medium gray or tan, and dark with black. Most often, I adjust the tension so the top thread pulls down toward the back slightly. This ensures against bobbin picking.

For embellishing, I like Kreinik's beautiful decorative threads, which include a wide array of metallics, blends, and twists, which you can use to add unique hand-stitched details to your work.

Needles

I use Microtex Sharp needles. I prefer the 80/12 but also use the 90/14 and 70/10 for different threads. Using the right needle makes a big difference in the raw-edge stitching. Changing needles often is also important to keep stitches looking their best.

Tear-Away Stabilizer

I use tear-away stabilizer to appliqué a block that will be in a large quilt. I raw-edge stitch all the blocks with tear-away stabilizer and then sash or join the project to make a complete top. For small projects, I simply fuse the whole top and baste the top to the batting with Mistyfuse. The batting acts as the stabilizer and gives the project some dimension, even before adding the backing and quilting it.

Mistyfuse

Basting is one of those things we all have to do but most of us dread. I have basted with pins. However, they are tough on your fingers, make quilts very heavy, and require putting all the pins in and taking all the pins out. I have also used a basting gun, which shoots plastic tacks through all three layers of a quilt. Those tacks also have to be removed and can leave large holes. Of course, you can hand baste, but this takes time, and the stitches also need to be removed. I do not use any of these methods anymore. Instead, I use Mistyfuse as my basting. Quilter Iris Karp of Attached Inc., in Brooklyn, New York, developed this amazing product. Mistyfuse is a very soft, light fusible product. It is like angel hair that is spread very thinly on a Christmas tree. The product does not behave like paper-backed fusible webbing, which can separate in heat and gum up in humidity. Mistyfuse comes in black and white and will not stiffen your project.

Batting

I like The Warm Company's Warm & Natural needled cotton batting. It has no resins or glues. It does not beard and can be quilted up to 10″ apart if you want to quilt lightly. I like the thin batting; in my experience, it sews easily. This product is dependable and washes well.

Work Space

I believe strongly in the value of having a clean work space. This saves time and results in the highest-quality finished project. If your work space is cluttered and dirty, you will spend more time looking for things and sorting than you do creating. I make it a point to tidy up each day after I am finished working; that way, I will be ready to start again with a clear mind the next time I get to work. Faced with a cluttered, disorganized space, I often do not want to start the project again. It can take a long time just to figure out where I left off.

Agra

Amsterdam

ATHENS

Auckland

Bangkok

Barcelona

Beijing 北京

Brussels

Budapest

Buenos Aires

CAIRO

Cape Town

CARIBBEAN

Dubai

Dublin

Edinburgh

Galápagos Islands

Geneva

香港
Hong Kong

Istanbul

JERUSALEM

WELCOME LAS VEGAS

Lima

London

Manila

Moscow

Munich

NAIROBI

NEW YORK

Oslo

Paris

Prague

PUERTO VALLARTA

Reykjavik

Rio De Janeiro

ROME

San Francisco

SAN JUAN

Seoul 서울

SINGAPORE

Sydney

Tokyo 日本

Toronto

VANCOUVER

Vatican City

Venice

Agra, India

Agra is a large city on the banks of the River Yamuna in central northern India, approximately 120 miles south of New Delhi, India's capital city. Agra has a humid subtropical climate with long, very hot summers; dry, cool winters; and monsoon in July and August. The city is a major tourist destination because of its many magnificent buildings, most notably the Taj Mahal, Agra Fort, and Fatehpur Sikri. The Taj Mahal is a world-famous mausoleum built by Mughal emperor Shah Jahan in memory of his third wife, Mumtaz Mahal, who died during the birth of their fourteenth child. Featuring Persian and Mughal architecture, it is one of the most beautiful buildings in the world, attracting between 2 million and 4 million visitors annually, and stands as a symbol of eternal love.

DIRECTIONS

Cut a 5½˝ × 6¾˝ rectangle for the sky (piece 1) and a 2½˝ × 6¾˝ rectangle for the land (piece 2). Leave excess to square and trim the block later. Sew the sky / land together with a ¼˝ seam to make the background. Position the sky / land by lining up the horizon line. Trace, cut, position, and fuse the remaining pieces in place. Small windows and details can be created with embroidery or fabric paint. After sewing the raw edges, trim and square the block to 6½˝ × 6½˝.

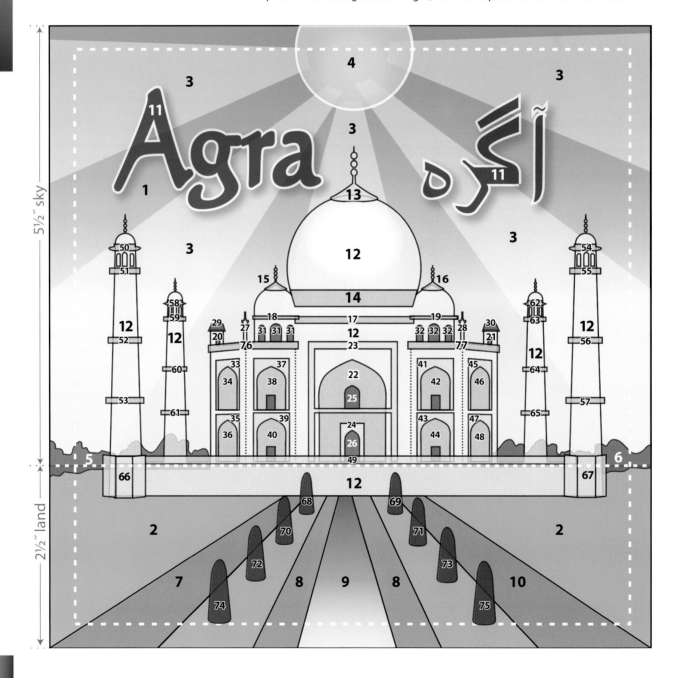

Amsterdam, the Netherlands

Amsterdam is nicknamed the "Venice of the North" for its hundreds of miles of canals, roughly 90 islands, and more than 1,500 bridges. The three main canals, dug in the seventeenth century and known as the Grachtengordel, form concentric beltways around the city. Amsterdam is the capital and largest city of the Netherlands and is in the province of North Holland. Main attractions include the historic canals, the Rijksmuseum, the Van Gogh Museum, the Stedelijk Museum, Hermitage Amsterdam, the Anne Frank House, the red-light district, and the many cannabis coffee shops. The North Sea and its prevailing northwesterly winds and gales influence Amsterdam's cool oceanic climate. Mild winter temperatures and moderately warm but rarely hot summers are common for this northern European city.

DIRECTIONS

Cut a 4½″ × 6¾″ rectangle for the sky (piece 1) and a 3½″ × 6¾″ rectangle for the land (piece 2). Leave excess to square and trim the block later. Sew the sky / land together with a ¼″ seam to make the background. Position the sky / land by lining up the horizon line. Trace, cut, position, and fuse the remaining pieces in place. Small windows and details can be created with embroidery or fabric paint. After sewing the raw edges, trim and square the block to 6½″ × 6½″.

Athens, Greece

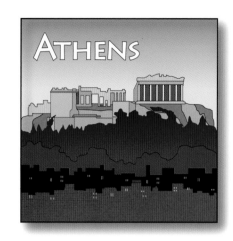

Athens is the capital and largest city of Greece. It is one of the world's oldest cities and is generally considered the birthplace of Western civilization. Athens endures hot summers, with extremely long periods of sunshine throughout the year. Winter is mild, with temperatures of 45–50°F, and snowfall is rare. Pericles built the Parthenon and other main buildings on the Acropolis as a monument in the fifth century B.C. The Acropolis is a flat-topped rock that rises almost 500 feet above sea level. Greece is at the southernmost tip of Europe and has one of the most unique geographic formations of any country in Europe.

DIRECTIONS

Cut a 4½″ × 6¾″ rectangle for the sky (piece 1) and a 3½″ × 6¾″ rectangle for the land (piece 2). Leave excess to square and trim the block later. Sew the sky / land together with a ¼″ seam to make the background. Position the sky / land by lining up the horizon line. Trace, cut, position, and fuse the remaining pieces in place. Small windows and details can be created with beading, embroidery, or fabric paint. After sewing the raw edges, trim and square the block to 6½″ × 6½″.

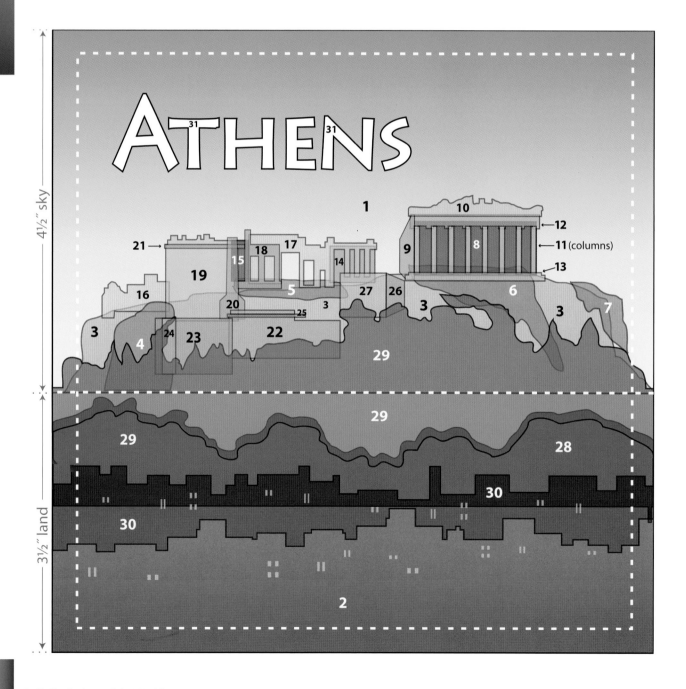

Auckland, New Zealand

Auckland, sometimes called the "City of Sails," is the largest city in New Zealand and is on an isthmus between the Hauraki Gulf of the Pacific Ocean to the east and the Waitakere Ranges to the west. The landscape boasts rich and fertile land made up of more than 40 volcanoes. Auckland has warm, wet summers and mild, damp winters. Auckland has the largest Polynesian population of any city in the world. The Sky Tower is a 1,076-foot-tall observation and telecommunications tower and an iconic structure in Auckland's skyline. The Sky Tower is the tallest freestanding structure in the Southern Hemisphere. Sheep are often seen grazing in the lush countryside and rich farmlands around the city. Beautiful landscapes and urban cultural areas make Auckland, New Zealand, a favorite tourist stop.

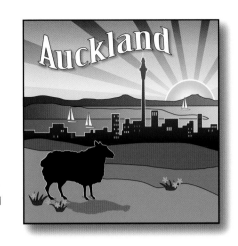

DIRECTIONS

Cut a 3½˝ × 6¾˝ rectangle for the sky (piece 1) and a 4½˝ × 6¾˝ rectangle for the land (piece 2). Leave excess to square and trim the block later. Sew the sky / land together with a ¼˝ seam to make the background. Position the sky / land by lining up the horizon line. Trace, cut, position, and fuse the remaining pieces in place. Small windows and details can be created with beading, embroidery, or fabric paint. Flowers can be created with novelty buttons. After sewing the raw edges, trim and square the block to 6½˝ × 6½˝.

Bangkok, Thailand

Bangkok, the "City of Angels," is the capital and largest city of Thailand. This eastern city has a hot, tropical climate with a rainy season that runs from May to October. Bangkok is known as the "Venice of the East" because of the number of canals and passages that divide the city. The Wat Phra Kaew, or the Temple of the Emerald Buddha, located in the Grand Palace, is revered as the most sacred Buddhist temple in Thailand. Housed inside is the precious 26-inch green statue that was carved from a single jade-colored precious stone. No one is allowed to touch the statue except for the Thai king, who changes the statue's fabric cloak three times a year.

DIRECTIONS

Cut a 4½″ × 6¾″ rectangle for the sky (piece 1) and a 3½″ × 6¾″ rectangle for the land (piece 2). Leave excess to square and trim the block later. Sew the sky / land together with a ¼″ seam to make the background. Position the sky / land by lining up the horizon line. Trace, cut, position, and fuse the remaining pieces in place. Small stars and details can be created with beading, embroidery, or fabric paint. The edges of the red roofs are green. I used a 1/8″ green ribbon for that detailing, sewn on by couching. You could also create the edge with a thick satin-stitch edging. You might need to sew 2 layers to get density. After sewing the raw edges, trim and square the block to 6½″ × 6½″.

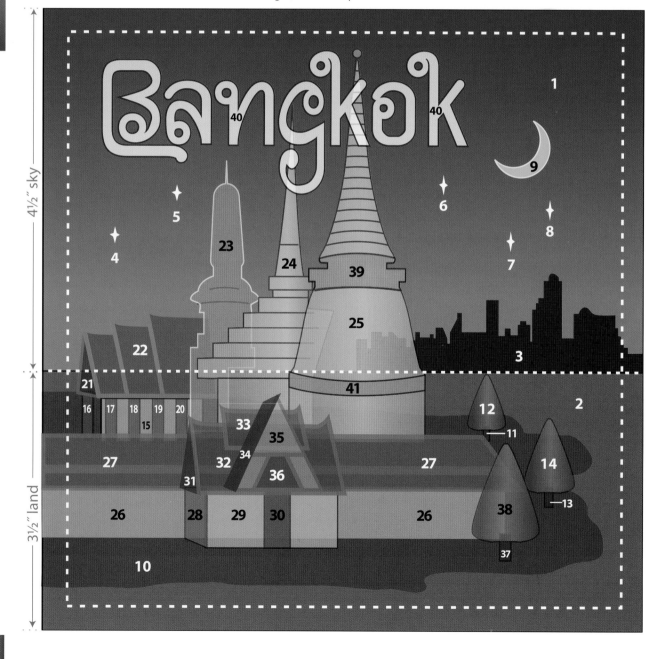

Barcelona, Spain

The "City of Counts" is an old nickname for Barcelona from Catalan history, based on the many counts that ruled from the ninth until the seventeenth century. This European city, on the Mediterranean Sea on the eastern coast of the Iberian Peninsula, has mild, humid winters and warm, dry summers. The Atlantic west winds often grace Barcelona with low humidity and little to no rain. Many of the buildings of this second-largest city in Spain date from medieval times. The Sagrada Família, designed by Spanish architect Antoni Gaudí (1852–1926), is a massive, privately funded Roman Catholic church that has been under construction since 1882, with a projected completion date as late as 2026.

DIRECTIONS

Cut a 4½″ × 6¾″ rectangle for the sky (piece 1) and a 3½″ × 6¾″ rectangle for the land (piece 2). Leave excess to square and trim the block later. Sew the sky/land together with a ¼″ seam to make the background. Position the sky/land by lining up the horizon line. Trace, cut, position, and fuse the remaining pieces in place. Small stars, windows, and details can be created with beading, embroidery, or fabric paint. After sewing the raw edges, trim and square the block to 6½″ × 6½″.

Beijing, China

Beijing, also known as Peking, is the capital of the People's Republic of China. The city's climate is hot and humid in summer and generally cold, windy, and dry in winter. Erosion of deserts results in seasonal dust storms that plague the city. Located in northern China, Beijing is renowned for its many opulent palaces, temples, and huge stone walls with gates. The Temple of Heaven is a complex of Taoist buildings visited over centuries by the emperors of the Ming and Qing dynasties to pray to heaven for good harvests. The Temple of Heaven was built in 1406–1420 completely from wood without the use of a single nail. The Great Wall of China was built across the mountains north of Beijing to guard against nomadic invasions. Beijing is one of the few cities in the world that has served as the political and cultural center of an area as large as China for so long.

DIRECTIONS

Cut a 4½″ × 6¾″ rectangle for the sky (piece 1) and a 3½″ × 6¾″ rectangle for the land (piece 2). Leave excess to square and trim the block later. Sew the sky/land together with a ¼″ seam to make the background. Position the sky/land by lining up the horizon line. Trace, cut, position, and fuse the remaining pieces in place. Small details can be created with beading, embroidery, or fabric paint. After sewing the raw edges, trim and square the block to 6½″ × 6½″.

Brussels, Belgium

Brussels, also known as "Comic City" and "Europe's Capital," is Belgium's capital city. During World War II people turned to comic strips for relief, and thus the first nickname was born. The second name refers to the fact that Brussels hosts many of the key institutions of the European Union. This beautiful city is near the Atlantic Ocean and a large wetland area, which provides an oceanic climate with approximately 200 days of rain per year. The Atomium, designed by André Waterkeyn, is a 335-foot-tall landmark in Brussels from the World Expo of 1958. It is a replica of an iron crystal enlarged 165 billion times. Visitors explore the unique structure, which provides a spectacular view of the city, art and science exhibitions, and a restaurant in its nine spheres. Brussels is renowned for its cultivation of brussels sprouts, Belgian chocolate, Belgian waffles, and many Belgian beers.

DIRECTIONS

Cut a 7½″ square for the background (piece 1). Leave excess to square and trim the block later. Trace, cut, position, and fuse the remaining pieces in place. Using silver lamé will give a metallic luster to the main iconic structure. Stabilize and use lower iron temperatures on specialty fabrics. After sewing the raw edges, trim and square the block to 6½″ × 6½″.

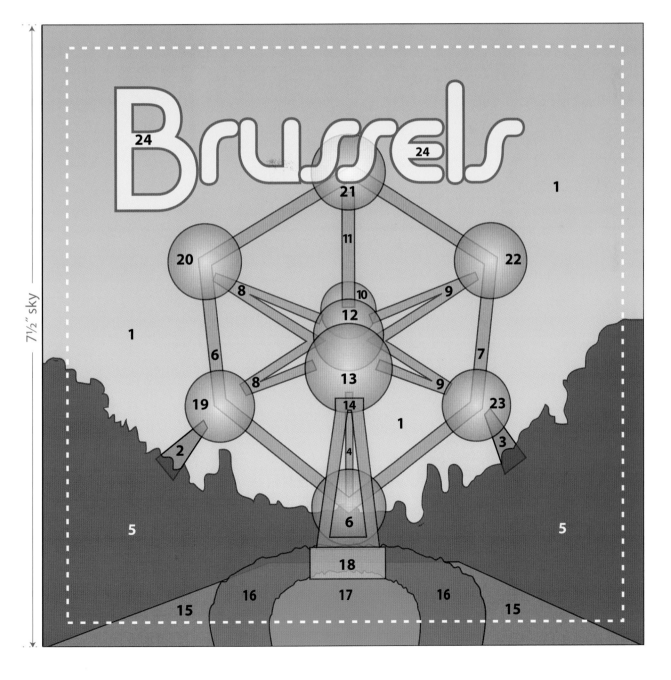

Budapest, Hungary

Budapest, the "Pearl of the Danube," is the picturesque riverside capital city of Hungary. The Hungarian Parliament Building in Lajos Kossuth Square is a notable landmark of this European country and a popular tourist destination. The Széchenyi Chain Bridge, the first permanent suspension bridge, which opened in 1849, spans the River Danube between Buda, the western side, and Pest, the eastern side of the city. When the bridge was built, it was among the most beautiful industrial monuments in Europe—a symbol of advancement and the link between the eastern and western sides of Budapest. The city has a temperate climate with mild winter weather and equally mild summers, with average temperatures in the mid to high seventies.

DIRECTIONS

Cut a 3½″ × 6¾″ rectangle for the sky (piece 1) and a 4½″ × 6¾″ rectangle for the land (piece 2). Leave excess to square and trim the block later. Sew the sky / land together with a ¼″ seam to make the background. Position the sky / land by lining up the horizon line. Trace, cut, position, and fuse the remaining pieces in place. Draw the bridge support wires with a fabric pen or pencil and straight stitch those elements. Pieces 10, 16, and 19 can be made from decorative lace. Small windows and details can be beaded, embroidered, or painted. After sewing the raw edges, trim and square the block to 6½″ × 6½″.

Buenos Aires, Argentina

Buenos Aires, the "Paris of the South," is the capital city of Argentina. It is the second-largest city in South America and is on the southeastern coast of the continent. Buenos Aires has a humid subtropical climate, with January being the warmest month and July the coolest. The Obelisk of Buenos Aires is an iconic national historic monument in the Plaza de la República. It was built to commemorate the fourth centennial of the city's founding. Buenos Aires boasts a wealth of history, architecture, and culture, with particular emphasis on the art of dancing, specifically the Argentine tango.

DIRECTIONS

Cut a 4½″ × 6¾″ rectangle for the sky (piece 1) and a 3½″ × 6¾″ rectangle for the land (piece 2). Leave excess to square and trim the block later. Sew the sky / land together with a ¼″ seam to make the background. Position the sky / land by lining up the horizon line. Trace, cut, position, and fuse the remaining pieces in place. Small windows and details can be beaded, embroidered, or painted. After sewing the raw edges, trim and square the block to 6½″ × 6½″.

Cairo, Egypt

The "City of a Thousand Minarets," Cairo is Africa's most populated city and Egypt's capital. Minarets are distinctive onion-shaped architectural crown features atop Islamic mosques. They provide a visual focal point and are used for the call to prayer. The weather in this northern African city is characterized by a desert climate but often with high humidity because of the Nile River valley's effects. The Great Sphinx and the pyramids in adjacent Giza are often associated with Cairo. The Great Pyramid of Khufu is the only one of the Seven Wonders of the Ancient World still remaining. Many believe it was a tomb built from 2584–2561 B.C. for the fourth-dynasty Egyptian pharaoh Khufu.

DIRECTIONS

Cut a 4½˝ × 6¾˝ rectangle for the sky (piece 1) and a 3½˝ × 6¾˝ rectangle for the land (piece 2). Leave excess to square and trim the block later. Sew the sky / land together with a ¼˝ seam to make the background. Position the sky / land by lining up the horizon line. Trace, cut, position, and fuse the remaining pieces in place. You might want to quilt or draw in the pyramid blocks. The points on the minarets can be embroidered or stitched. After sewing the raw edges, trim and square the block to 6½˝ × 6½˝.

Cape Town, South Africa

Weary sailors needing to relax after being on a ship for months at a time coined "Tavern of the Sea" long ago as a nickname for Cape Town. This popular tourist destination is known for its wide diversity of cultures and languages. Cape Town enjoys a subtropical Mediterranean climate with mild, wet winters and dry, hot summers. Table Mountain and Cape Point are the recognizable land formations behind the City Bowl. Table Mountain is flanked by the near-vertical cliffs of Devil's Peak and Lion's Head and is often draped in a narrow strip of clouds locally referred to as the "tablecloth." Cape Peninsula National Park is home to many African penguins, which can be found on long stretches of rocky and sandy shorelines.

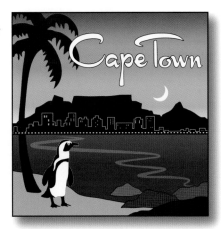

DIRECTIONS

Cut a 4½″ × 6¾″ rectangle for the sky (piece 1) and a 3½″ × 6¾″ rectangle for the land (piece 2). Leave excess to square and trim the block later. Sew the sky/land together with a ¼″ seam to make the background. Position the sky/land by lining up the horizon line. Trace, cut, position, and fuse the remaining pieces in place. Raw-edge appliquéing the skyline with neon green thread makes the city appear to be lit up. Tiny windows in the skyline can be made with beads, embroidery, or fabric paint. After sewing the raw edges, trim and square the block to 6½″ × 6½″.

Caribbean

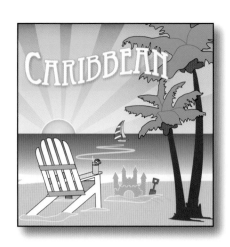

The West Indies, often simply called the Caribbean, is a subregion of North America in the Caribbean Sea, southeast of Mexico. This tropical paradise is made up of more than 7,000 islands, islets, reefs, and cays. The largest of these islands are Cuba, Haiti, the Dominican Republic, Jamaica, Puerto Rico, Trinidad, Guadeloupe, and Martinique. The islands are varied geographically, with some being very flat and others quite mountainous. The year-round tropical climate and incredible blue seas make it a popular destination for millions of tourists. The Caribbean is directly in the weather path of many hurricanes during the summer months. The West Indies boast of their spectacular scuba diving and snorkeling spots with vibrantly colored tropical fish.

DIRECTIONS

Cut a 4½″ × 6¾″ rectangle for the sky (piece 1) and a 3½″ × 6¾″ rectangle for the land (piece 2). Leave excess to square and trim the block later. Sew the sky / land together with a ¼″ seam to make the background. Position the sky / land by lining up the horizon line. Trace, cut, position, and fuse the remaining pieces in place. The small tropical cocktail can be made with fabric paint. Included on the CD are nine alternate patterns of popular island names in the area that you might want to use instead of "Caribbean." After sewing the raw edges, trim and square the block to 6½″ × 6½″.

Dubai, United Arab Emirates

Dubai, nicknamed the "City of Gold," is one of the seven emirates of the United Arab Emirates (UAE). South of the Persian Gulf on the Arabian Peninsula within the Arabian Desert, Dubai is an affluent global city built on the oil industry, banking, and tourism. Dubai has an impressive city skyline, with the Burj Khalifa (Khalifa or Dubai Tower), which is the world's tallest building at 2,716.5 feet, completed in 2010. The iconic Burj Al Arab, designed to symbolize Dubai's urban transformation, is a deluxe luxury hotel in the shape of a sailboat that stands on an artificial island. The city has a plethora of amazing buildings and man-made island areas.

DIRECTIONS

Cut a 4½˝ × 6¾˝ rectangle for the sky (piece 1) and a 3½˝ × 6¾˝ rectangle for the land (piece 2). Leave excess to square and trim the block later. Sew the sky / land together with a ¼˝ seam to make the background. Position the sky / land by lining up the horizon line. Trace, cut, position, and fuse the remaining pieces in place. The small details and windows can be created with beading, fabric paint, or embroidery. The striped portion of the hotel in the front can be made with striped fabric. Sewing the raw edges around the skyline with neon green thread will make the city look like it is lit up. After sewing the raw edges, trim and square the block to 6½˝ × 6½˝.

Dublin, Ireland

Dublin (meaning "black pool") is the largest and capital city of Ireland, housing almost 25 percent of the nation's population. The modern Irish name for the city is Baile Átha Cliath, meaning "town of the hurdled ford." It is near the midpoint of the country's east coast, at the mouth of the River Liffey. To the south, Dublin is bordered by a low mountain range, and to the north and west are flat farmlands. Dublin has cool summers and mild winters, with an absence of temperature extremes. King John of England orderd Dublin Castle built as a major defensive project in 1204 after the Norman invasion of Ireland in 1169. The castle used the River Poddle as a natural means of defense to protect the king's treasures. Dublin has produced many prominent literary figures, including Yeats, Shaw, Beckett, Wilde, Joyce, Swift, and Stoker.

DIRECTIONS

Cut a 4½″ × 6¾″ rectangle for the sky (piece 1) and a 3½″ × 6¾″ rectangle for the land (piece 2). Leave excess to square and trim the block later. Sew the sky / land together with a ¼″ seam to make the background. Position the sky / land by lining up the horizon line. Trace, cut, position, and fuse the remaining pieces in place. The small details and windows can be created with beading, fabric paint, or embroidery. After sewing the raw edges, trim and square the block to 6½″ × 6½″.

Edinburgh, Scotland

Edinburgh, the "Athens of the North," is the capital city of Scotland. It has a relatively mild climate despite its northerly location. Winters are very mild, and summers are generally moderate. The city's landscape is a result of early volcanic activity and periods of intense glaciation more than 350 million years ago. Castle Rock, located on a volcanic plug, is one of Scotland's notable landmarks. With a ravine to the south, this volcanic formation was an ideal natural fortress, upon which Edinburgh Castle was built. The rugged setting and medieval and Georgian stone architecture draw millions of visitors to this part of Europe.

DIRECTIONS

Cut a 4½″ × 6¾″ rectangle for the sky (piece 1) and a 3½″ × 6¾″ rectangle for the land (piece 2). Leave excess to square and trim the block later. Sew the sky / land together with a ¼″ seam to make the background. Position the sky / land by lining up the horizon line. Trace, cut, position, and fuse the remaining pieces in place. The small details and windows can be created with beading, fabric paint, or embroidery. After sewing the raw edges, trim and square the block to 6½″ × 6½″.

Galápagos Islands, Ecuador

The Galápagos Islands, nicknamed the "Enchanted Islands," are a cluster of volcanic islands near the equator in the Pacific Ocean off the west coast of South America. There are fifteen main islands, three smaller islands, and many small rocks and islets. The equatorial location makes these islands quite warm year-round, with very wet conditions on volcanic mountaintops caused by altitude temperature changes. Pinnacle Rock is the most famous land formation in the Galápagos. It is a large, stately, black eroded lava formation created when the magma expelled from a volcano on Bartolomé Island reached the sea. The Galápagos' most notable feature, especially near Pinnacle Rock, is wildlife, including iguanas, giant tortoises, sea cucumbers, blue-footed boobies, penguins, albatrosses, and Galápagos sea lions.

DIRECTIONS

Cut a 4½″ × 6¾″ rectangle for the sky (piece 1) and a 3½″ × 6¾″ rectangle for the land (piece 2). Leave excess to square and trim the block later. Sew the sky / land together with a ¼″ seam to make the background. Position the sky / land by lining up the horizon line. Trace, cut, position, and fuse the remaining pieces in place. The small details of the tortoise can be created with fabric paint or marker. After sewing the raw edges, trim and square the block to 6½″ × 6½″.

Geneva, Switzerland

Geneva, or the "Peace Capital," is at the southwestern end of Lake Geneva, where the lake flows back into the Rhône River. It is surrounded by two mountain chains, the Alps and the Jura. Crescent-shaped Lake Geneva is central Europe's largest freshwater lake. Located on Lake Geneva is Chillon Castle, or Château de Chillon, one of Switzerland's most visited destinations, first recorded historically around 1160. Geneva is a global city recognized as a strong financial center as well as a leader in diplomacy. Geneva enjoys a temperate climate, with winters that are moderate (despite excellent skiing in the mountains) and summers that are warm.

DIRECTIONS

Cut a 4½˝ × 6¾˝ rectangle for the sky (piece 1) and a 3½˝ × 6¾˝ rectangle for the land (piece 2). Leave excess to square and trim the block later. Sew the sky / land together with a ¼˝ seam to make the background. Position the sky / land by lining up the horizon line. Trace, cut, position, and fuse the remaining pieces in place. The small windows and details can be created with embroidery, fabric paint, or marker. After sewing the raw edges, trim and square the block to 6½˝ × 6½˝.

Hong Kong

Renowned for its deep natural harbor, steep mountains, and expansive skyline, Hong Kong is often referred to as "The World's Most Vertical City." It has more than 7,500 skyscrapers. The tallest building to date, at 108 stories, is the International Commerce Centre, completed in 2010, overlooking Victoria Harbor. Located on the south coast of China, Hong Kong is known as a "special administrative region" of the country. Seven million people make this city one of the most densely populated in the world. Tourists visit the famous giant bronze statue of Tian Tan Buddha on Lantau Island. It is one of the largest outdoor Buddha statues in the world. Many tourists also stop to see Mickey Mouse in Hong Kong Disneyland on the same island. Hong Kong has a humid subtropical climate with hot summers and very mild winters.

DIRECTIONS

Cut a 3½″ × 6¾″ rectangle for the sky (piece 1) and a 4½″ × 6¾″ rectangle for the land (piece 2). Leave excess to square and trim the block later. Sew the sky/land together with a ¼″ seam to make the background. Position the sky/land by lining up the horizon line. Trace, cut, position, and fuse the remaining pieces in place. The small windows and details can be created with embroidery, fabric paint, or marker. Facial features and cloth wrinkles can be stitched or drawn with fabric marker. After sewing the raw edges, trim and square the block to 6½″ × 6½″.

Istanbul, Turkey

Istanbul, historically known as Constantinople or Byzantium, is the largest city in Turkey and one of the largest cities in the world, with a population of around 13 million people. It straddles two continents, Europe and Asia. The Istanbul Strait, also known as the Bosphorus Strait, is a narrow waterway that connects the Black Sea with the Sea of Marmara. The Golden Horn is a natural harbor that further divides the city. One of Istanbul's famous landmarks, the Blue Mosque, was completed in 1616 and is known for its decorative interior of blue Byzantine tiles, although its exterior is gray. This massive, majestic mosque has six minarets, many dome roofs, and an open courtyard that faces the Hagia Sophia Museum. Istanbul has a Mediterranean climate with quite a bit of morning sea fog. It has hot summers and wet, cold winters.

DIRECTIONS

Cut a 4½″ × 6¾″ rectangle for the sky (piece 1) and a 3½″ × 6¾″ rectangle for the land (piece 2). Leave excess to square and trim the block later. Sew the sky / land together with a ¼″ seam to make the background. Position the sky / land by lining up the horizon line. Trace, cut, position, and fuse the remaining pieces in place. The small windows and star details can be created with embroidery, fabric paint, or marker. After sewing the raw edges, trim and square the block to 6½″ × 6½″.

Jerusalem, Israel

Jerusalem, the "City of Peace," is the capital and largest city of Israel. In the Judean Mountains, between the Mediterranean Sea and the northern edge of the Dead Sea, this is the holiest of cities to the three main Abrahamic religions—Judaism, Christianity, and Islam. Many travel to Israel to visit the Wailing Wall, which is and has been a famous site for Jewish prayer and pilgrimage for centuries. The Tower of David houses archaeological artifacts dating back 2,700 years. The Dome of the Rock is an Islamic shrine and major landmark on the Temple Mount in Jerusalem. Completed in 691–692, it is one of the oldest existing Islamic buildings in the world. The city experiences hot, dry summers and mild, wet winters, with snow once or twice a winter.

DIRECTIONS

Cut a 4½″ × 6¾″ rectangle for the sky (piece 1) and a 3½″ × 6¾″ rectangle for the land (piece 2). Leave excess to square and trim the block later. Sew the sky/land together with a ¼″ seam to make the background. Position the sky/land by lining up the horizon line. Trace, cut, position, and fuse the remaining pieces in place. The small windows, stars, and wall details can be created with embroidery, fabric paint, or marker. After sewing the raw edges, trim and square the block to 6½″ × 6½″.

Las Vegas, USA

Otherwise known as "Sin City," Las Vegas has become an international resort destination known for gambling, shopping, fine dining, and family fun. The famous welcome sign, designed by Betty Willis, is a Las Vegas Strip landmark. The city is more than 2,000 feet above sea level in the arid Mojave Desert. The city enjoys an average of 300 sunny days per year. The summers are very hot, with average daytime highs of 94°–104°F. Winters are short and warm. Millions visit each year from all corners of the world. Of course, we all know…"What happens in Vegas stays in Vegas!"

DIRECTIONS

Cut a 4½″ × 6¾″ rectangle for the sky (piece 1) and a 3½″ × 6¾″ rectangle for the land (piece 2). Leave excess to square and trim the block later. Sew the sky/land together with a ¼″ seam to make the background. Position the sky/land by lining up the horizon line. Trace, cut, position, and fuse the remaining pieces in place. The small windows, stars, and other details can be created with embroidery, fabric paint, or marker. Stitching around the city silhouettes with neon green thread will make the city look lit up. Using beads or fusible crystals would be fitting for this block. After sewing the raw edges, trim and square the block to 6½″ × 6½″. The Las Vegas sign is available for photo-fabric printing on the CD.

Lima, Peru

Lima, the "City of Kings," is the capital and largest city of Peru. It is in a desert in the central part of the country overlooking the Pacific Ocean. The river that feeds Lima is called Rímac, a name with Incan roots, meaning "Talking River." The Basilica Cathedral is in the Plaza Mayor of downtown Lima and is one of the nation's most important landmarks. Construction began in 1535 and was consecrated in 1625. This national landmark was designed by Francisco Pizarro, who conquered the Incas and founded Lima. Basilica Cathedral houses fine baroque art and contains Pizarro's tomb. The location on the Pacific Ocean gives Lima a comfortable subtropical climate even though the city is in the tropics and in a desert. Temperatures range between 50°F and 85°F throughout the year.

DIRECTIONS

Cut a 4½″ × 6¾″ rectangle for the sky (piece 1) and a 3½″ × 6¾″ rectangle for the land (piece 2). Leave excess to square and trim the block later. Sew the sky/land together with a ¼″ seam to make the background. Position the sky/land by lining up the horizon line. Trace, cut, position, and fuse the remaining pieces in place. The small windows and other details can be created with embroidery, fabric paint, or marker. Using beads or decorative flower buttons would be very effective on this block. After sewing the raw edges, trim and square the block to 6½″ × 6½″.

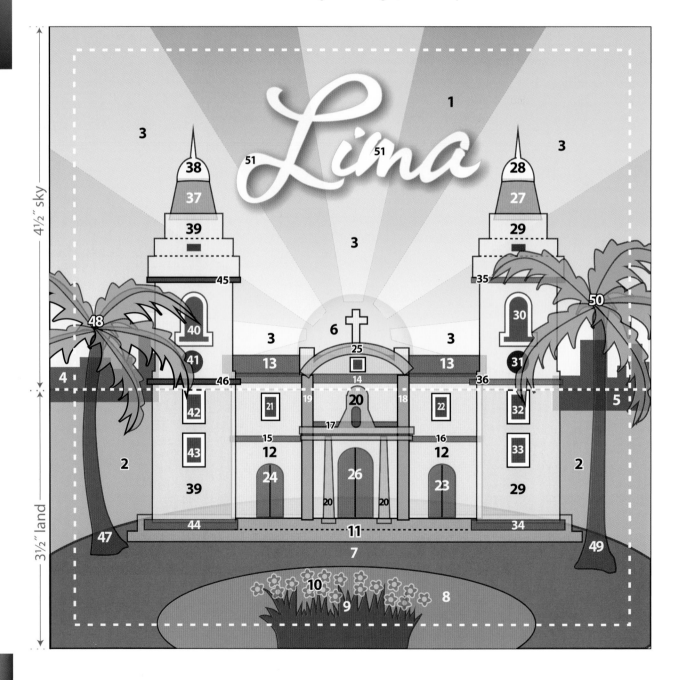

London, England

"The Big Smoke" is London's little-known nickname. London's famed familiar fog and the Great Smog of 1952 that killed thousands are said to be the nickname's origin. The temperatures of England's capital are classified as marine climate. The summer months average 73°F, with a 10° range up or down. Winters in London are chilly but rarely below freezing. Surprisingly, London is considered a dry city, with regular but generally very light precipitation throughout the year. London has a rich history going back more than 2,000 years. The British royal family, the House of Windsor, resides in world-famous Buckingham Palace in London. Other notable landmarks are the Tower Bridge, Tower of London, the London Eye (the world's largest Ferris wheel), Westminster Palace, St. Paul's Cathedral, and the inspirational Thames River.

DIRECTIONS

Cut a 3½˝ × 6¾˝ rectangle for the sky (piece 1) and a 4½˝ × 6¾˝ rectangle for the land (piece 2). Leave excess to square and trim the block later. Sew the sky / land together with a ¼˝ seam to make the background. Position the sky / land by lining up the horizon line. Trace, cut, position, and fuse the remaining pieces in place. The small windows and other details can be created with embroidery, fabric paint, or marker. After sewing the raw edges, trim and square the block to 6½˝ × 6½˝.

Manila, the Philippines

Manila, the "Pearl of the Orient," is the capital city of the Philippines, and is located on the eastern shores of Manila Bay. Manila has a tropical wet and dry climate with annual temperatures that are generally quite humid and warm because of its proximity to the equator. January through April is considered the dry season, with a lengthy wet season from May through December. Tourism in Manila attracts more than 1 million visitors each year. Major destinations include the 1322 Golden Empire Tower, Intramuros, the Mendiola, Rizal Park, and the Manila Cathedral. The Manila Cathedral, also known as the Metropolitan Cathedral-Basilica, has been damaged or destroyed several times since the original cathedral was built in 1581. It is dedicated to the Patroness of the Philippines, Blessed Virgin Mary, under the title Our Lady of the Immaculate Conception.

DIRECTIONS

Cut a 4½″ × 6¾″ rectangle for the sky (piece 1) and a 3½″ × 6¾″ rectangle for the land (piece 2). Leave excess to square and trim the block later. Sew the sky / land together with a ¼″ seam to make the background. Position the sky / land by lining up the horizon line. Trace, cut, position, and fuse the remaining pieces in place. The small windows and other details can be created with embroidery, fabric paint, or marker. After sewing the raw edges, trim and square the block to 6½″ × 6½″.

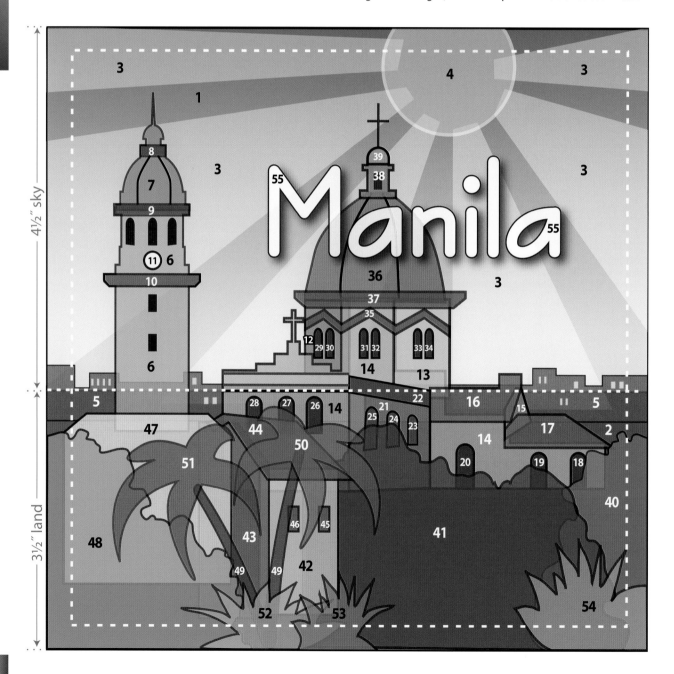

Moscow, Russia

At one time Moscow was referred to as "the Kremlin," meaning fortress or castle. It is Russia's pulse center, housing the Russian government (and formerly the Soviet government). This European city is on the Moskva River, west of the Ural Mountains. The city has a humid climate with gentle, warm summers and long, cold winters. The average annual temperature in Moscow is 42°F. The famous Russian Orthodox cathedral St. Basil's is in Red Square. It was founded in 1555 by Ivan IV and designed by Barma and Postnik. St. Basil's Cathedral is one of the world's most unique architectural structures, with its flame-shaped towers mimicking fire rising into the sky.

DIRECTIONS

Cut a 4½″ × 6¾″ rectangle for the sky (piece 1) and a 3½″ × 6¾″ rectangle for the land (piece 2). Leave excess to square and trim the block later. Sew the sky / land together with a ¼″ seam to make the background. Position the sky / land by lining up the horizon line. Trace, cut, position, and fuse the remaining pieces in place. The small windows and other details can be created with embroidery, fabric paint, or marker. The scalloped trim can be created using decorative lace. After sewing the raw edges, trim and square the block to 6½″ × 6½″. This block has many pieces. Go slow and be patient.

Munich, Germany

Munich, nicknamed "Gateway of the Bavarian Alps," is the capital city of Bavaria, Germany, and is on the River Isar north of the Bavarian Alps. The city's motto is "Munich likes you." Located at a relatively high altitude and sprawling into the foothills of the Alps, the city receives ample precipitation from many rainstorms, which are often violent and unexpected. Munich experiences cold winters and moderate summers with an average temperature of 73°F. Munich is renowned for its architecture and culture. The annual Oktoberfest beer celebration is world famous. The Hofbräuhaus am Platzl is a beer hall in the city center built in 1598 as an extension of the original Hofbräu Brewery.

DIRECTIONS

Cut a 4½″ × 6¾″ rectangle for the sky (piece 1) and a 3½″ × 6¾″ rectangle for the land (piece 2). Leave excess to square and trim the block later. Sew the sky / land together with a ¼″ seam to make the background. Position the sky / land by lining up the horizon line. Trace, cut, position, and fuse the remaining pieces in place. The small windows and other details can be created with embroidery, fabric paint, or marker. After sewing the raw edges, trim and square the block to 6½″ × 6½″.

Nairobi, Kenya

Nairobi, which comes from a phrase meaning "the place of cool waters," is the capital and largest city of Kenya. Nairobi has two nicknames: the "Green City in the Sun," for its foliage and warm climate, and the "Safari Capital of the World," for its world-renowned safari vacations. The famous Nairobi National Park is the only game reserve to border a capital city of this size. Nairobi has a subtropical highland climate. The altitude allows Nairobi to have cool evenings, but its close proximity to the equator makes for very warm days and little seasonal climate change. Mount Kenya is north of Nairobi, and Mount Kilimanjaro is toward the southeast. Both mountains are visible from Nairobi on a clear day. Kilimanjaro is an extinct volcano, formed several million years ago; it is in Mount Kenya National Park.

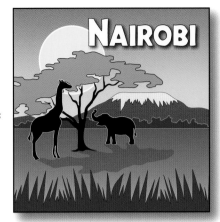

DIRECTIONS

Cut a 4½″ × 6¾″ rectangle for the sky (piece 1) and a 3½″ × 6¾″ rectangle for the land (piece 2). Leave excess to square and trim the block later. Sew the sky/land together with a ¼″ seam to make the background. Position the sky/land by lining up the horizon line. Trace, cut, position, and fuse the remaining pieces in place. The animal shadow can be created with dark tulle or organza. After sewing the raw edges, trim and square the block to 6½″ × 6½″.

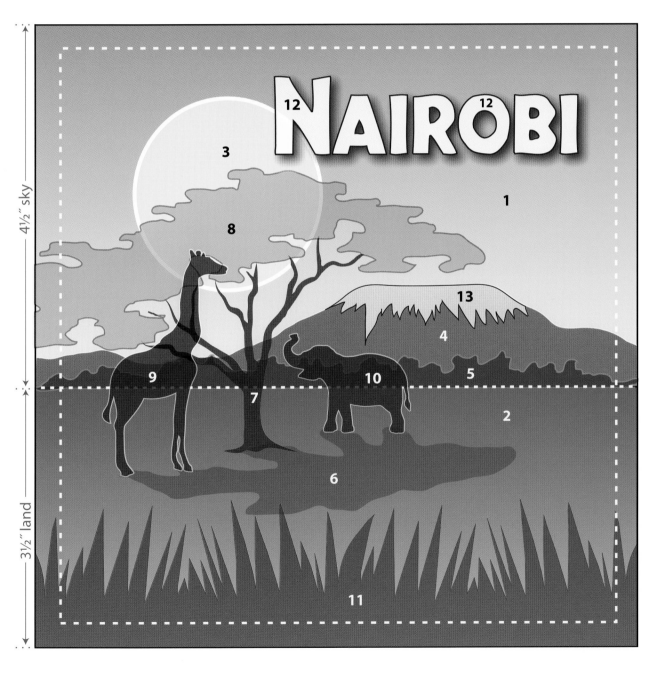

New York City, USA

The "Big Apple," New York is a leading global city with powerful influence in global commerce, culture, art, fashion, research, education, and entertainment. It is on the East Coast of the United States of America. The city experiences four full seasons, with very warm summer temperatures and winters that are cold and often snowy. New York Harbor's Statue of Liberty greeted millions of immigrants as they came to America in the late nineteenth century. The monument commemorates the centennial of the signing of the U.S. Declaration of Independence and was given to the United States by the people of France. Other notable landmarks include the Brooklyn Bridge, the Chrysler Building, the Citicorp Building, Broadway, many museums, Wall Street, Central Park, and the former site of the World Trade Center.

DIRECTIONS

Cut a 4½″ × 6¾″ rectangle for the sky (piece 1) and a 3½″ × 6¾″ rectangle for the land (piece 2). Leave excess to square and trim the block later. Sew the sky / land together with a ¼″ seam to make the background. Position the sky / land by lining up the horizon line. Trace, cut, position, and fuse the remaining pieces in place. The small windows and details can be created with fabric paint, embroidery, or beading. The statue face can be drawn with fabric markers. After sewing the raw edges, trim and square the block to 6½″ × 6½″.

Oslo, Norway

Oslo is the capital of and largest city in Norway. Oslo, meaning "the meadow at the foot of the hill," is surrounded by hills and mountains, with approximately 40 islands and over 300 lakes, which are the main source of drinking water for the city. Despite its northerly location, the climate is relatively mild because of the Gulf Stream. Oslo has gentle summers and long, cold, snowy winters. The Oslo Opera House was completed in 2007 and features opera, ballet, music and dance theater, and concerts. The angled exterior surfaces of the building are covered with Italian marble, white granite, glass, and metal, which make it appear to rise from the water like an iceberg. The unique Atlantic puffin, with its bright orange beak and feet, can be seen in large colonies along Norwegian coastlines.

DIRECTIONS

Cut a 4½″ × 6¾″ rectangle for the sky (piece 1) and a 3½″ × 6¾″ rectangle for the land (piece 2). Leave excess to square and trim the block later. Sew the sky / land together with a ¼″ seam to make the background. Position the sky / land by lining up the horizon line. Trace, cut, position, and fuse the remaining pieces in place. The shadows can be created with dark tulle or organza. The puffin eye can be drawn with fabric markers or embroidered. After sewing the raw edges, trim and square the block to 6½″ × 6½″.

Paris, France

The "City of Light" is one of the most visited cities in the world. Paris is the largest city in France. It has one of the lowest rainfall averages in France, but the city is known for its unexpected rain showers at any time of year. Summer temperatures are warm, with occasional heat waves, while winters are cold, with temperatures hovering around freezing. Earliest history claims Paris was founded about 250 B.C. by a Celtic tribe called the Parisii, who fished from their dugout canoes on the Seine River, which passes through Paris. Notable landmarks are the Louvre, the Sacré-Cœur Basilica, Notre Dame Cathedral, and, of course, the Eiffel Tower.

DIRECTIONS

Cut a 4½˝ × 6¾˝ rectangle for the sky (piece 1) and a 3½˝ × 6¾˝ rectangle for the land (piece 2). Leave excess to square and trim the block later. Sew the sky / land together with a ¼˝ seam to make the background. Position the sky / land by lining up the horizon line. Trace, cut, position, and fuse the remaining pieces in place. The small windows and details (#10) can be painted, beaded, or embroidered. Lace is an interesting alternative for some of the building pieces (#11). After sewing the raw edges, trim and square the block to 6½˝ × 6½˝.

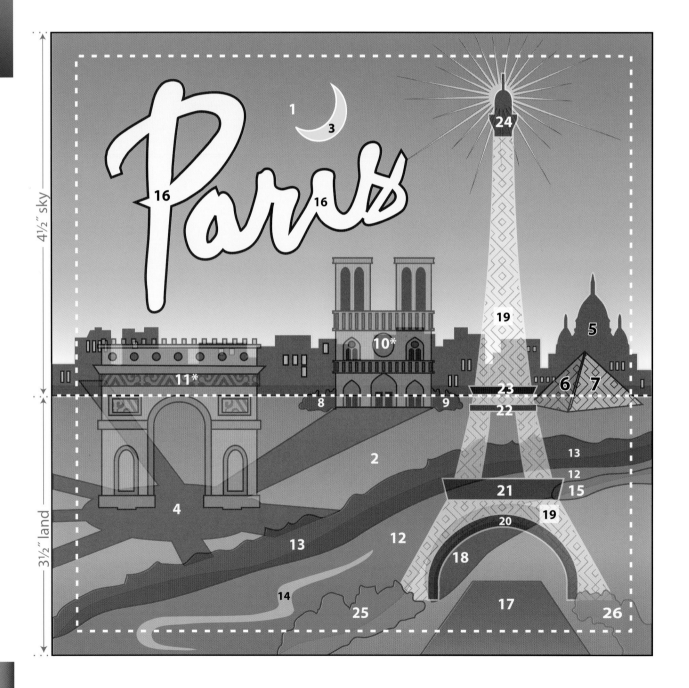

Prague, the Czech Republic

Prague, nicknamed the "Mother of Cities," is the capital and largest city of the Czech Republic. It is one of Europe's top tourist destinations. Prague is in Bohemia, a region of the Czech Republic just west of the country's center. The Vltava River, which runs north to south through this landlocked country, bisects Prague and its Old Town. Some of the best-known landmarks in the city are the Prague Castle (one of the largest castles in the world), St. Vitus cathedral, the famous Old Town Square with the astronomical clock, and the picturesque Charles Bridge spanning the Vltava River. Construction on the Charles Bridge, originally called the Stone Bridge, began in 1357 under King Charles IV and was not completed until 1402. Prague, also referred to as the "City of a Hundred Spires," has a varied climate throughout the year, with hot summers and cloudy, cold winters.

DIRECTIONS

Cut a 4½″ × 6¾″ rectangle for the sky (piece 1) and a 3½″ × 6¾″ rectangle for the land (piece 2). Leave excess to square and trim the block later. Sew the sky / land together with a ¼″ seam to make the background. Position the sky / land by lining up the horizon line. Trace, cut, position, and fuse the remaining pieces in place. The small windows and details can be painted, beaded, or embroidered. After sewing the raw edges, trim and square the block to 6½″ × 6½″.

Puerto Vallarta, Mexico

Puerto Vallarta, also called "PV" or simply "Vallarta," is a popular Mexican resort city on the Pacific Ocean's Bay of Banderas. Puerto Vallarta was named after Ignacio Vallarta, a former governor of the state of Jalisco, Mexico, where PV is located. The Cathedral of Our Lady of Guadalupe is the city's most notable landmark. The interior of the Catholic cathedral is filled with hand-carved columns, decorative moldings, and rich detailing. Rafael Zamarripa's seahorse sculpture on the popular Malecón (or boardwalk) has become the symbol of the city. It is a nine-foot bronze statue of a naked boy riding on the sea creature's back. The climate in PV is tropical wet, with a very dry season in the winter. The summers can be very hot and extremely humid.

DIRECTIONS

Cut a 4½˝ × 6¾˝ rectangle for the sky (piece 1) and a 3½˝ × 6¾˝ rectangle for the land (piece 2). Leave excess to square and trim the block later. Sew the sky / land together with a ¼˝ seam to make the background. Position the sky / land by lining up the horizon line. Trace, cut, position, and fuse the remaining pieces in place. The small windows and details can be painted, beaded, or embroidered. After sewing the raw edges, trim and square the block to 6½˝ × 6½˝.

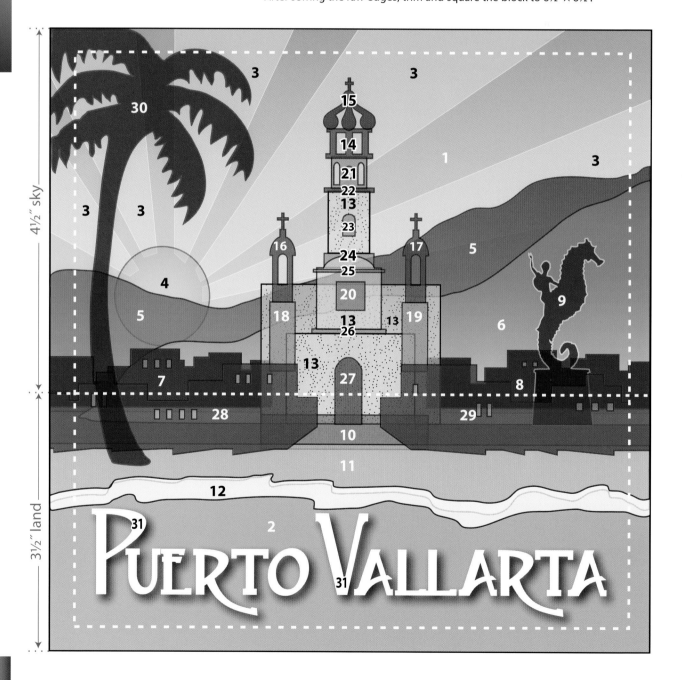

Reykjavik, Iceland

Reykjavik, the capital of Iceland, is in the country's southwest, on the southern shore of Faxaflói Bay. Steam from hot springs in the region is supposed to have inspired Reykjavik's name, which means "Bay of Smokes." The city was founded in 1786 as an official trading town. The Reykjavik-area coastline is made up of peninsulas, coves, straits, and islands. The climate is subpolar oceanic, with summers that are cool and windy and winters that are cold and snowy. One of Reykjavik's most imposing and notable landmarks is the Church of Hallgrimur. It is a Lutheran parish church and observatory that soars 244 feet into the Icelandic sky. After 38 years under construction, the church was completed in 1986. It houses a massive organ with more than 5,000 pipes. The church was designed to resemble the basalt lava flows of Iceland's landscape.

DIRECTIONS

Cut a 4½″ × 6¾″ rectangle for the sky (piece 1) and a 3½″ × 6¾″ rectangle for the land (piece 2). Leave excess to square and trim the block later. Sew the sky/land together with a ¼″ seam to make the background. Position the sky/land by lining up the horizon line. Trace, cut, position, and fuse the remaining pieces in place. The small windows and details can be painted, beaded, or embroidered. The icy spots on the type could be enhanced with opalescent fabric glitter. After sewing the raw edges, trim and square the block to 6½″ × 6½″.

Rio de Janeiro, Brazil

Rio de Janeiro, nicknamed "Marvelous City," is well known for its beautiful beaches, its carnival celebrations, and its giant statue, Christ the Redeemer, atop Corcovado Mountain overlooking the city and sea. This famous art deco statue soars 130 feet high in Brazil's Tijuca Forest on the Atlantic coast and Guanabara Bay. This iconic symbol of Rio is made from reinforced concrete and soapstone. It took almost ten years to build and was completed in 1930. In 2007, Christ the Redeemer was named one of the New Seven Wonders of the World. Rio enjoys a warm tropical climate with heavy rain in the winter months. This picturesque seaside city is Brazil's main tourist destination and boasts many historic cathedrals and museums.

DIRECTIONS

Cut a 3½″ × 6¾″ rectangle for the sky (piece 1) and a 4½″ × 6¾″ rectangle for the land (piece 2). Leave excess to square and trim the block later. Sew the sky / land together with a ¼″ seam to make the background. Position the sky / land by lining up the horizon line. Trace, cut, position, and fuse the remaining pieces in place. The small windows and details can be painted, beaded, or embroidered. After sewing the raw edges, trim and square the block to 6½″ × 6½″.

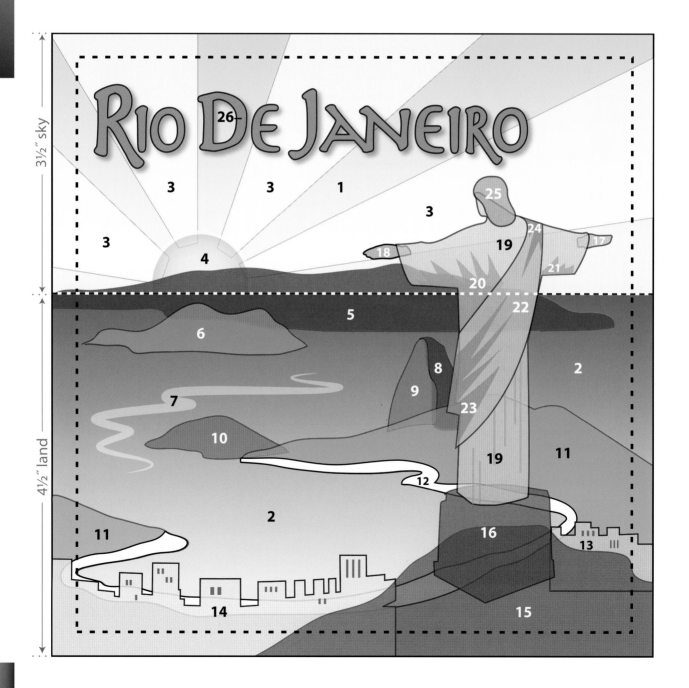

Rome, Italy

Rome, also known as the "Eternal City," is in the central-western portion of the Italian penin-sula, on the Tiber River. Rome is the capital of Italy and has a history spanning more than 2,500 years. The Colosseum, with seating for 50,000, was used for gladiator contests and other public spectacles; it is considered one of the greatest works of Roman architecture and engineering. Its construction started around A.D. 70 under the emperor Vespasian and was completed in A.D. 80 under Titus. The Pantheon, the ancient temple that was initially dedicated to all the gods, and Santa Maria Maggiore, one of the most ancient churches in the world, are must-see tourist stops. Most of the year Rome enjoys moderate to warm weather with mild winters.

DIRECTIONS

Cut a 4½″ × 6¾″ rectangle for the sky (piece 1) and a 3½″ × 6¾″ rectangle for the land (piece 2). Leave excess to square and trim the block later. Sew the sky / land together with a ¼″ seam to make the background. Position the sky / land by lining up the horizon line. Trace, cut, position, and fuse the remaining pieces in place. The small windows and details can be painted or embroidered. After sewing the raw edges, trim and square the block to 6½″ × 6½″. Note: You could cut all windows from piece 9 and back whole piece where windows show with dark brown.

San Francisco, USA

San Francisco, or the "City by the Bay," is home to the world-famous Golden Gate Bridge, cable cars, steep rolling hills, and Chinatown. This popular California tourist city, named after St. Francis of Assisi, is renowned for its eclectic mix of Victorian and modern architecture. San Francisco's rows of "Painted Ladies," a term used for Victorian homes that are embellished with three or more vivid colors enhancing their architectural details, make for an enchanting sight. The city is on the west coast of the United States and is surrounded on three sides by water. The climate is coastal, with mild, wet winters and cool, dry summers. San Francisco's weather is strongly influenced by the Pacific Ocean, which produces a mild year-round climate with little seasonal temperature variation and frequent foggy conditions on the bay.

DIRECTIONS

Cut a 4½″ × 6¾″ rectangle for the sky (piece 1) and a 3½″ × 6¾″ rectangle for the land (piece 2). Leave excess to square and trim the block later. Sew the sky/land together with a ¼″ seam to make the background. Position the sky/land by lining up the horizon line. Trace, cut, position, and fuse the remaining pieces in place. The small windows and details can be painted or embroidered. The cross pieces on houses should be created with decorative lace. After sewing the raw edges, trim and square the block to 6½″ × 6½″.

San Juan, Puerto Rico

San Juan, founded in 1521 by Juan Ponce de León, is the capital of Puerto Rico, an unincorporated territory of the United States. San Juan is an important seaport and financial, cultural, and tourism center. Historically, San Juan was used as a stopover by ships traveling from Spain to the Americas. The city is along the northeastern coast of Puerto Rico, on San Juan Bay. The garita, or sentry box, is one of Puerto Rico's most recognized symbols. The iconic garitas lined the Old San Juan walls and forts that warded off enemy attacks and protected the city. San Juan enjoys a tropical climate, with temperatures ranging from 70°F to 90°F throughout the year.

DIRECTIONS

Cut a 4½″ × 6¾″ rectangle for the sky (piece 1) and a 3½″ × 6¾″ rectangle for the land (piece 2). Leave excess to square and trim the block later. Sew the sky / land together with a ¼″ seam to make the background. Position the sky / land by lining up the horizon line. Trace, cut, position, and fuse the remaining pieces in place. The small windows and details can be painted or embroidered. Transfer and stitch the dome lines to make the dome appear curved. After sewing the raw edges, trim and square the block to 6½″ × 6½″.

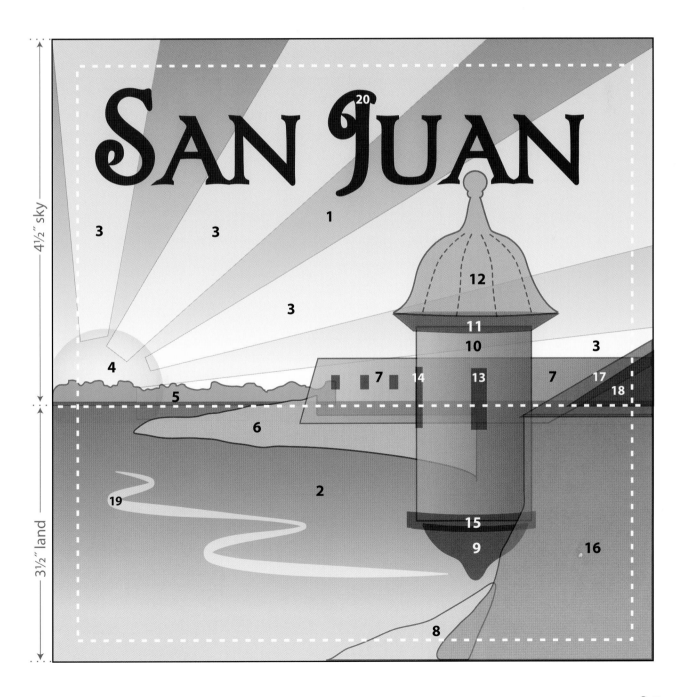

Seoul, South Korea

"Seoul" means "capital city." It is the capital and largest city of South Korea. Namdaemun, meaning "the south gate," was erected in 1398 and is Seoul's oldest wood-built structure. While popularly called Namdaemun, the gate is officially called the "Sungnyemun" (Gate of Exalted Ceremonies) and is a historic pagoda-style gateway in the center of Seoul. The nation has listed Namdaemun first among the National Treasures of South Korea since 1962. The structure fell victim to arson in 2008 and is being restored. Seoul is in northwest South Korea and is bisected by the Han River. Eight mountains, as well as the Han River plain, border the city. Summers are generally hot and humid, with monsoons in June and July. Winters are cold, with an average of 28 days of snow annually.

DIRECTIONS

Cut a 4½″ × 6¾″ rectangle for the sky (piece 1) and a 3½″ × 6¾″ rectangle for the land (piece 2). Leave excess to square and trim the block later. Sew the sky / land together with a ¼″ seam to make the background. Position the sky / land by lining up the horizon line. Trace, cut, position, and fuse the remaining pieces in place. After sewing the raw edges, trim and square the block to 6½″ × 6½″.

Singapore

Singapore is a Southeast Asian city-state between Malaysia and Indonesia. Singapore was founded as a British trading colony in 1819. It joined the Malaysian Federation in 1963 but then separated two years later and became independent. It is a highly urbanized island country 85 miles north of the equator. Singapore, which is made up of 63 islands, was a notable trading hub centuries ago and remains an important trade site today. The "Lion City" has a tropical rain-forest climate with high humidity and abundant rainfall but does not have significant seasonal changes; temperatures range from 75°F to 95°F year-round. The mythical symbol of Singapore is the merlion, a cross between a fish and a lion that spouts water from its mouth. There are five official Merlion statues in Singapore, but the original is in Merlion Park at Marina Bay.

DIRECTIONS

Cut a 4½″ × 6¾″ rectangle for the sky (piece 1) and a 3½″ × 6¾″ rectangle for the land (piece 2). Leave excess to square and trim the block later. Sew the sky / land together with a ¼″ seam to make the background. Position the sky / land by lining up the horizon line. Trace, cut, position, and fuse the remaining pieces in place. Small windows and details can be created with embroidery, fabric paint, or beading. Lion details can be created by stitching or with fabric markers. After sewing the raw edges, trim and square the block to 6½″ × 6½″.

Sydney, Australia

Sydney, "Harbour City," is the largest city in and the state capital of New South Wales, Australia. Sydney is on the southeast coast of the Tasman Sea. Sydney has a temperate climate with warm summers and cool winters. The warmest month is January, with an average temperature of 65–78°F. The coldest month is July, with an average temperature of 46–61°F. Snow is extremely rare in Sydney. The iconic Sydney Opera House, designed by architect Jørn Utzon, and the Harbour Bridge are two of the most famous "down under" landmarks. Queen Elizabeth II, queen of Australia, opened the Opera House in 1973. The Harbour Bridge, the world's overall largest steel arch bridge, opened in March 1932 and is often referred to by locals as "the Coat Hanger."

DIRECTIONS

Cut a 4½″ × 6¾″ rectangle for the sky (piece 1) and a 3½″ × 6¾″ rectangle for the land (piece 2). Leave excess to square and trim the block later. Sew the sky / land together with a ¼″ seam to make the background. Position the sky / land by lining up the horizon line. Trace, cut, position, and fuse the remaining pieces in place. Small windows and details can be created with fabric paint, embroidery, or beading. Sun rays are optional and can be made from tulle or organza. After sewing the raw edges, trim and square the block to 6½″ × 6½″.

Tokyo, Japan

Tokyo, originally known as Edo, meaning "estuary," changed its name to Tokyo—to ("east") + kyo ("capital")—when it became Japan's capital in 1868. Tokyo is on the eastern side of the main island, Honshu. It is the largest metropolitan area of Japan and home to the imperial family. Tokyo has a humid subtropical climate with hot, humid summers and generally mild winters with some cold spells. Mount Fuji, an active volcano that last erupted in 1707–1708, is just west of Tokyo and can be seen from the city on a clear day. Tokyo's current cityscape is one of modern and contemporary architecture. Older buildings are scarce because of the 1923 Great Kanto Earthquake and the subsequent extensive firebombing in World War II, which destroyed much of the historic architecture.

DIRECTIONS

Cut a 4½″ × 6¾″ rectangle for the sky (piece 1) and a 3½″ × 6¾″ rectangle for the land (piece 2). Leave excess to square and trim the block later. Sew the sky / land together with a ¼″ seam to make the background. Position the sky / land by lining up the horizon line. Trace, cut, position, and fuse the remaining pieces in place. Small windows and details can be created with fabric paint, embroidery, or beading. After sewing the raw edges, trim and square the block to 6½″ × 6½″.

Toronto, Canada

"TO," "Muddy York," "T-dot," "Hog City," or "Queen City"—take your pick of all these nicknames for Toronto, the capital of Ontario. TO is the largest city in Canada and is on the northwestern shore of Lake Ontario. This urban part of southern Ontario, known as the Golden Horseshoe, is home to approximately 25 percent of Canada's population. The CN (Canadian National) Tower, completed in 1976, is a communications and observation tower that is currently the tallest structure in the Western Hemisphere. Toronto is a booming international city, with more skyscrapers being added every year. The city has four distinct seasons, including warm, humid summers and cold winters. Lake Ontario greatly influences the climate with lake-effect snow, fog, and the delaying of spring- and fall-like conditions, known as seasonal lag.

DIRECTIONS

Cut a 4½″ × 6¾″ rectangle for the sky (piece 1) and a 3½″ × 6¾″ rectangle for the land (piece 2). Leave excess to square and trim the block later. Sew the sky/land together with a ¼″ seam to make the background. Position the sky/land by lining up the horizon line. Trace, cut, position, and fuse the remaining pieces in place. Small windows and details can be created with fabric paint, embroidery, or beading. After sewing the raw edges, trim and square the block to 6½″ × 6½″.

Vancouver, Canada

Vancouver was named for British captain George Vancouver, who founded the coastal city in British Columbia in the 1790s. Vancouver has earned the nickname "Hollywood North" because so many U.S. movies are filmed in this beautiful Canadian city. The city is on the Burrard Peninsula, with the North Shore Mountains as a picturesque backdrop. The Fraser River is to the south and the Strait of Georgia is to the west, next to the Pacific Ocean. The climate is coastal and temperate, with summers that are moderately warm and dry. Most days during late fall and winter are rainy but with relatively little snowfall. Vancouver's climate is one of Canada's mildest. The Inukshuk (a stone landmark built by Arctic-region natives of North America) at Stanley Park has been identified with Vancouver ever since the city hosted the 2010 Olympic Games. This icon was designated the games' official symbol.

DIRECTIONS

Cut a 4½″ × 6¾″ rectangle for the sky (piece 1) and a 3½″ × 6¾″ rectangle for the land (piece 2). Leave excess to square and trim the block later. Sew the sky / land together with a ¼″ seam to make the background. Position the sky / land by lining up the horizon line. Trace, cut, position, and fuse the remaining pieces in place. Small windows and details can be created with fabric paint, embroidery, or beading. After sewing the raw edges, trim and square the block to 6½″ × 6½″.

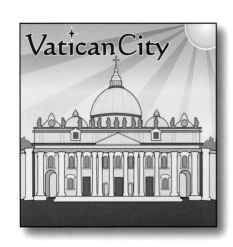

Vatican City

Vatican City is an ecclesiastical walled city within Rome, Italy, that covers an area of approximately 110 acres. With a population of just more than 800 residents, it is the world's smallest country. Italian is the country's official language. Established in 1929 by the Lateran Treaty, this landlocked sovereign city-state is ruled by the Bishop of Rome—the pope. Features of this religious state include the Vatican Gardens, which make up almost half of the entire city's area and are filled with beautiful fountains, sculptures, and vegetation; the pope's residence in the Apostolic Palace, near St. Peter's Square; St. Peter's Basilica; and the Sistine Chapel, which houses some of the most famous art in the world, including works by Bramante, Botticelli, Raphael, Bernini, and Michelangelo. Vatican City, has mild, rainy winters from September to mid-May and hot, dry summers from May to August.

DIRECTIONS

Cut a 4½˝ × 6¾˝ rectangle for the sky (piece 1) and a 3½˝ × 6¾˝ rectangle for the land (piece 2). Leave excess to square and trim the block later. Sew the sky / land together with a ¼˝ seam to make the background. Position the sky / land by lining up the horizon line. Trace, cut, position, and fuse the remaining pieces in place. Small windows and details can be created with fabric paint, embroidery, or beading. After sewing the raw edges, trim and square the block to 6½˝ × 6½˝.

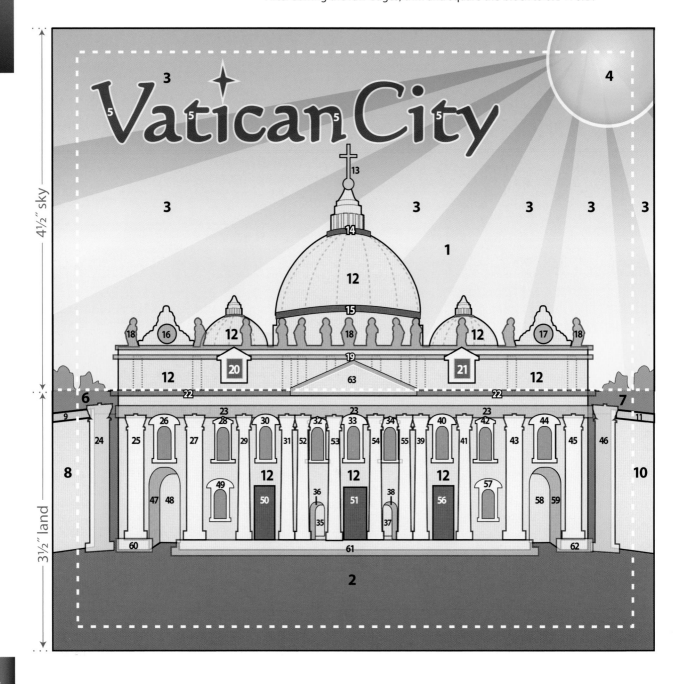

Venice, Italy

Venice, the "Floating City," in northern Italy is known for tourism and industry. The Rialto Bridge, one of more than 400 bridges in the city, arches over the Grand Canal in the heart of the Rialto area, which is famous for its popular fruit and vegetable market. The city lies across 117 small islands in the marshy Venetian Lagoon along the Adriatic Sea. Venice has a humid subtropical climate with cool winters and hot summers. This city offers beautiful landscapes, art, and a rich history that draws a huge tourist population. Venice is home to St. Mark's Basilica, the Grand Canal, and Piazza San Marco. Transportation within the city remains, as it was in centuries past, entirely by water or by foot. The classic Venetian boat is the gondola, which is used mostly for tourists, weddings, funerals, or other ceremonies. The locals use water taxis or private boats.

DIRECTIONS

Cut a 4½″ × 6¾″ rectangle for the sky (piece 1) and a 3½″ × 6¾″ rectangle for the land (piece 2). Leave excess to square and trim the block later. Sew the sky / land together with a ¼″ seam to make the background. Position the sky / land by lining up the horizon line. Trace, cut, position, and fuse the remaining pieces in place. Small windows and details can be created with fabric paint, embroidery, or beading. After sewing the raw edges, trim and square the block to 6½″ × 6½″.

Around the World Block, 12″ × 12″

Bucket List Block, 12″ × 12″

Traveling Gabel Family Block, 12″ × 12″

Where We've Been Block, 12″ × 12″

Around the World

Our world is approximately 8,000 miles in diameter, with a circumference of about 24,900 miles; oceans cover about 71 percent of the Earth's surface. Just how many countries are in our world? That answer is complex. Because the world is made up of states, territories, colonies, and other nondescript geographic areas, it is difficult to determine an exact number. Some characterize a "country" as being a defined area that is an official member of the United Nations. Based on that criterion, there are 192 countries. Others, using a broader definition of the term, believe there are more than 250 countries. The political climate of this world is ever changing, which makes that an ever-changing number. Use this block to illustrate your travels—or aspirations for travel— Around the World!

DIRECTIONS

This block has a solid 7″ × 7″ background, unlike most of the other blocks in this book. Cut a square 7″ × 7″ for the background. Trace, cut, position, and fuse the remaining pieces in place. The dotted airplane trail can be hand sewn with heavy decorative or perle cotton thread. Small details can be created with fabric paint, embroidery, or beading. After sewing the raw edges, trim and square the block to 6½″ × 6½″.

7″ background

Bucket List

Our world is approximately 8,000 miles in diameter, with a circumference of about 24,900 miles; oceans cover about 71 percent of the Earth's surface. Just how many countries are in our world? That answer is complex. Because the world is made up of states, territories, colonies, and other nondescript geographic areas, it is difficult to determine an exact number. Some characterize a "country" as being a defined area that is an official member of the United Nations. Based on that criterion, there are 192 countries. Others, using a broader definition of the term, believe there are more than 250 countries. The political climate of this world is ever changing, which makes that an ever-changing number. We live in a big, wonderful world. We would all love to see some of these amazing destinations. What world locations would be on you bucket list?

DIRECTIONS

Cut a 3½″ × 6¾″ rectangle for the sky (piece 1) and a 4½″ × 6¾″ rectangle for the land (piece 2). Leave excess to square and trim the block later. Sew the sky / land together with a ¼″ seam to make the background. Position the sky / land by lining up the horizon line. Trace, cut, position, and fuse the remaining pieces in place. Small details can be created with fabric paint, embroidery, or beading. After sewing the raw edges, trim and square the block to 6½″ × 6½″.

Traveling Family

Our world is approximately 8,000 miles in diameter, with a circumference of about 24,900 miles; oceans cover about 71 percent of the Earth's surface. Just how many countries are in our world? That answer is complex. Because the world is made up of states, territories, colonies, and other nondescript geographic areas, it is difficult to determine an exact number. Some characterize a "country" as being a defined area that is an official member of the United Nations. Based on that criterion, there are 192 countries. Others, using a broader definition, believe there are more than 250 countries. The political climate of this world is ever changing, which makes that an ever-changing number.

DIRECTIONS

Cut a 3½˝ × 6¾˝ rectangle for the sky (piece 1) and a 4½˝ × 6¾˝ rectangle for the land (piece 2). Leave excess to square and trim the block later. Sew the sky / land together with a ¼˝ seam to make the background. Position the sky / land by lining up the horizon line. Trace, cut, position, and fuse the remaining pieces in place. Use the alphabet on the CD to customize this block. Small details can be created with fabric paint, embroidery, or beading. After sewing the raw edges, trim and square the block to 6½˝ × 6½˝.

Where We've Been!

Our world is approximately 8,000 miles in diameter, with a circumference of about 24,900 miles; oceans cover about 71 percent of the Earth's surface. Just how many countries are in our world? That answer is complex. Because the world is made up of states, territories, colonies, and other nondescript geographic areas, it is difficult to determine an exact number. Some characterize a "country" as being a defined area that is an official member of the United Nations. Based on that criterion, there are 192 countries. Others, using a broader definition, believe there are more than 250 countries. The political climate of this world is ever changing, which makes that an ever-changing number. This block is the ultimate answer in fabric to the question, "Where ya been?"

DIRECTIONS

This block has a solid 7″ × 7″ background, unlike most of the other blocks in this book. Cut a square 7″ × 7″ for the background. Trace, cut, position, and fuse the remaining pieces in place. You could use decorative buttons or embroidery to highlight your destinations instead of star patterns. After sewing the raw edges, trim and square the block to 6½″ × 6½″.

7″ background

London Town, 12″ × 12″
by Linda K. Bernard

Beijing, 14″ × 14″
by Cynthia Porter

Munich, 15″ × 15″
by Linda K. Bernard

Prague, 17½″ × 17½″
by Linda K. Bernard

Munich, 12½″ × 12½″
by Linda K. Bernard

Amsterdam / Embroidery, 18″ × 17″
by Lee Hofstetter

Honeymoon, 13″ × 47″
by Monica Agapaloglou

Munich pillow, 16″ × 11″
by Lee Hofstetter

British Isles, 27″ × 60″
by Genie Corbin

Vancouver wall bowl
by Mindy Williams

Beaches Around the World scrapbook cover, 8″ × 8″
by Lee Hofstetter

Tokyo
by Lee Hofstetter

It's a Small World, 12″ × 18″ × 8″
by Lee Hofstetter

Caribbean, 12″ × 14″ × 6″
by Karen Moss

Tokyo, 18″ × 20″ × 6″
by Ruth Erickson

London on Canvas, 20″ × 20″
by Amy Morusiewicz

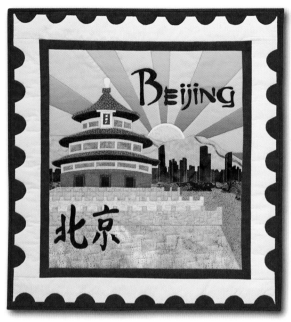

Beijing Stamp
by Lee Zadareky

Around the World, 47″ × 77″
by Misty Cole

Toronto, 14″ × 18″
by Lee Hofstetter

Auckland Block, 12″ × 12″

Manila Block, 12″ × 12″

Buenos Aires Block, 12″ × 12″

Moscow Block, 12″ × 12″

Galápagos Islands Block, 12″ × 12″

Munich Block, 12″ × 12″

Oslo Block, 12″ × 12″

Seoul Block, 12″ × 12″

Puerto Vallarta Block, 12″ × 12″

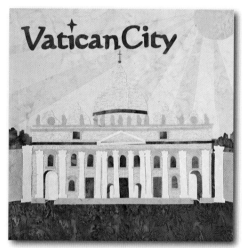

Vatican City Block, 12″ × 12″

Rio de Janeiro Block, 12″ × 12″

Venice Block, 12″ × 12″

Bangkok Block, 12″ × 12″

Amsterdam Block, 12″ × 12″

Vancouver Block, 12″ × 12″

Agra Block, 12″ × 12″

Reykjavik Block, 12″ × 12″

Hong Kong Heritage, 48″ × 48″
by Genie Corbin

Supplies and Resources

Listed below are the manufacturers and sources of supplies and materials recommended throughout the book. These are for your information in the event that you would like to try them out.

Attached Inc. (Mistyfuse and Fat Goddess Sheets)

60 Washington Avenue
Brooklyn, NY 11205
631.750.8500
www.mistyfuse.com

Hoffman California Fabrics (batiks and other fine fabrics)

25792 Obrero Drive
Mission Viejo, CA 92691
800.547.0100
www.hoffmanfabrics.com

Kiwi Quilt Studio (official Zebra Patterns sample maker)

Patti Rusk – Custom Quiltmaker
6616 Kilmarnoch Drive
Catonsville, MD 21228
plrusk@msn.com
410.852.0676

Kreinik (decorative and specialty threads)

1708 Gihon Road
Parkersburg, WV 26102
800.537.2166
www.kreinik.com

Pangor Design Quilt Studio (longarm quilting services)

Maria O'Haver
Ellicott City, MD
410.750.3866
maria@mariaohaver.com

Thread Works Studio (official Zebra Patterns sample maker)

Mindy Williams – Custom Quiltmaker
30 Saratoga Drive
New Castle, DE 19720
302.545.7859
threadworksmindy@comcast.net

The Warm Company (batting and fusible webbing)

5529 186th Place SW
Lynnwood, WA 98037
425.248.2424
www.warmcompany.com

YLI (threads)

1439 Dave Lyle Boulevard, #16C
Rock Hill, SC 29730
803.985.3100
www.ylicorp.com

Zebra Patterns (Debra Gabel's pattern company)

Debra Gabel
13618 Meadow Glenn
Clarksville, MD 21029
410.370.3798
www.zebrapatterns.com

For a list of other fine books from C&T Publishing, ask for a free catalog:

C&T Publishing, Inc.
P.O. Box 1456
Lafayette, CA 94549
800-284-1114
Email: ctinfo@ctpub.com
Website: www.ctpub.com

Tips and Techniques can be found at www.ctpub.com > Consumer Resources > Quiltmaking Basics: Tips & Techniques for Quiltmaking & More

C&T Publishing's professional photography services are now available to the public. Visit us at www.ctmediaservices.com.

For quilting supplies:

Cotton Patch
1025 Brown Ave.
Lafayette, CA 94549
Store: 925-284-1177
Mail order: 925-283-7883
Email: CottonPa@aol.com
Website: www.quiltusa.com

Note: Fabrics shown may not be currently available, as fabric manufacturers keep most fabrics in print for only a short time.

About the Author

Born in Middletown, New York, Debra started sewing as a child and quilting as a teen. After several professional moves around the United States in adulthood, she finally settled in Clarksville, Maryland, with her husband, Gary, and their three sons, Brooks, Austin, and Cole. Armed with a bachelor of fine arts in graphic design, Debra worked for many years as an art director in the packaging industry, where she designed and prepared art for paper-handled shopping bags, consumer goods, tissue, decorative boxes, and other packaging. Debra has also maintained her independent graphic design business, Mixed Media, since 1988.

After rediscovering quilting in the late 1990s, Debra started teaching quilting locally in 2000. Her classes were based on patterns she had designed for baby quilt gifts and a simple Christmas stocking pattern. The popularity of the classes and the interest in the patterns were the start of a small pattern line and additional part-time teaching opportunities.

In 2003, at age 42, Debra was shocked to be diagnosed with non-Hodgkin's lymphoma, late stage three. It was a trying time for the whole family. Rigorous chemotherapy began in August, concluded in November, and was followed by an autologous (self-donor) bone marrow stem cell transplant on December 26. Released from Baltimore's Johns Hopkins Hospital in January 2004 with a new lease on life, Debra began the slow process of an almost two-year recovery.

It was a time of deep reflection. All the time in and out of the hospital—with endless days spent in bed and losing friends and acquaintances met during treatments at Johns Hopkins—gave her ample time to review her life and think about what might be her future. Inspired by the words of Oprah Winfrey, she decided to *follow her passions*—quilting and design—and to shoot for the moon. The first goal during that recovery period was simple: to regain the basic independence of getting up and getting dressed by herself each day. Over time, the plan to give serious effort to being a pattern designer was firmly established.

Debra started thinking about a name for her new pattern company. As a graphic designer, Debra loves bold colors and black and white. She particularly likes black and white stripes. Since her name is Debra, she decided to replace the "D" with a "Z," and Zebra Patterns was born.

Since the first few patterns designed in her precancer days, Debra has steadily built up her quilt pattern line to include 30 beautiful florals, 12 birds, 12 butterflies, 12 Bible stories, more than 70 signature stamps, a woven bias floral series, several baby quilts, and many unique quilted projects and art quilts. Debra currently teaches and lectures at guilds and quilt shops in the United States, while regularly adding new patterns and products to the Zebra Patterns line.

Debra also has had success entering and showing her quilts in regional and national quilt shows; has had her quilts appear in calendars, quilt books, and websites; and has been featured in and authored magazine articles.

Debra intends to continue lecturing, teaching, and evolving as a quilter, speaker, and author. She would like to travel the world through quilting. Debra has a website that showcases all her art quilts, her patterns, and an extensive ongoing blog called "Shoot for the Moon." Debra's blog tells the stories of her current activities—quilting and then some—and is a resource for quilters wanting to follow their passion with a pattern line of their own. Visit **www.zebrapatterns.com** for the blog and much, much more.

Also by Debra Gabel:

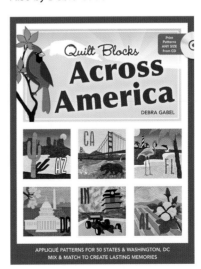

Great Titles & Products *from* C&T PUBLISHING & STASH BOOKS

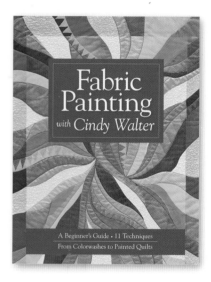

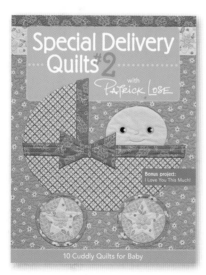

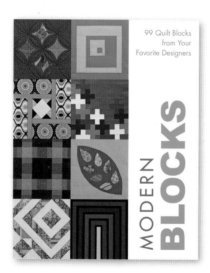

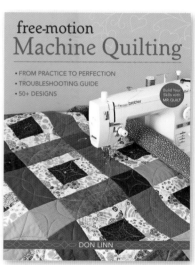

Available at your local retailer or **www.ctpub.com** *or* **800-284-1114**